That My Family
Should Partake

Neal A. Maxwell

That My Family Should Partake

Published by Deseret Book Company
Salt Lake City, Utah
1974

Lithographed by

DESERET PRESS

in the United States of America

Dedication

This book is respectfully dedicated to prospective parents
and to young parents everywhere, with the sincere desire
that what little wisdom lies within these pages may help
them in a small way as they face the challenges of
parenthood, and with the hope that the successes and the
imperfections of the "outgoing" generation of parents may
help the "incoming" generation of parents (to use Moroni's
words) "learn to be more wise than we have been."
(Moroni 9:31.)

Contents

Acknowledgments

The author expresses appreciation to his General Authority colleagues who have shared insightful wisdom from their own family experiences in comments and letters to the author, particularly in Chapter 5; to W. James Mortimer of Deseret Book for his patient encouragement of the author to undertake these "after hours" tasks; to Laura Castano for both her friendship and secretarial support; to Elizabeth Haglund and Dr. Blaine Porter, who were kind enough to read and to react to the manuscript, making wise and candid suggestions; and to Eleanor Knowles for her editorship. Appreciation to President Henry B. Eyring of Ricks College for catalytic conversations and to Dick Hazelett and Tony Kimball for sharing their own ideas as well as their finds from the world of books.

Gratitude is expressed also to readers (that slim band on the spectrum of the reading population), whose comments on my past efforts provided some momentum for this effort, and to Colleen, Becky, Mike, Cory, Nancy, and Jane for reactions, anecdotes, and their emotional "advance" that underwrote this venture.

CHAPTER ONE

Inasmuch as Parents Have Children

The title for this volume comes from the words of Lehi (1 Nephi 8:12) where, having partaken of the fruit of "the tree which is precious above all," Lehi's soul was filled "with exceeding great joy." Then Lehi began, as all good parents should, "to be desirous that my family should partake of it also." Parents who have, through gospel living, partaken of the fruit of the tree (which is the love of God) and who know the sweet sense of surrender in the kingdom of God will also be stirred, as Lehi was, for they too will be anxious, exceedingly anxious, that their families should partake also. Those who have known the sweetness of service in the kingdom and who have looked at life through the lens of the gospel will ever be restless with a divine discontent until their families do partake of that precious fruit and thereby witness for themselves.

It is equally significant, however, that the words in this book's title are those of a father, Lehi, who did not have automatic, or total, success with his own family. Lehi experienced some of the failures and frustrations that sometimes go with family life.

1

Most of us, in a sense, experience three families in a lifetime: the first, the family in which we ourselves are reared; second, the family in which we serve as a parent; third, the larger family in which we experience the joys—and challenges—of grandparenthood. It is a rare parent who has not known, especially in his second family, those anguished moments when he is desperately anxious to communicate to his children those things of great value and to communicate clearly about the things he truly cherishes.

President Harold B. Lee said it well when he said that the most important work we will ever do is the work we do within the walls of our own home. Given such a challenge, it is not surprising that sincere parents are anxious to make their house a home and not merely a hotel—where mother is maid and chef and father is a desk clerk and a bell captain with the car keys.

Most parents, along with the real and recurring joys of parenthood, will also know those moments experienced by Father Lehi, who described himself as "a trembling parent" and who found it necessary to speak in pure exhortation to his children "with all the feelings of a tender parent."

All parents should be grateful for those models about us of parents who, though they have other church, civic, and community roles that matter, show us by their words and actions that they know they have no more important assignment under heaven than as parents. Yet too much multiplication of other roles can divide our effectiveness at home.

We should be grateful not only for living models, but also for model families in the past, such as that of Joseph Smith, Sr., who, along with his wife, Lucy Mack Smith, gave a boy prophet love, leadership, example, and support. Suppose, after walking back from that theophany at Palmyra, young Joseph Smith had encountered task-oriented ("Get the chores done!"), nonlistening parents? Or a jealous older brother? With all else he had to meet in the way of ridicule and persecution, could that lad have done his special work without the love and courage of a family that quietly, uncomplainingly agreed to share in his work and in his fate?

Just as certain people must be prepared to do God's work, so, too, families are prepared beforehand to host special individuals—like the family of yet another Joseph wherein the Savior himself was reared!

The home is so crucial that it is the source of our greatest failures as well as our greatest joys. It is one place that presses us to practice every major gospel principle, not just a few as may be the case in some fleeting and temporary relationships.

Life in a family means we are known as we are, that our frailties are exposed and, hopefully, we then correct them.

The affection and thoughtfulness required in the home are no abstract exercises in love, no mere rhetoric concerning some distant human cause. Family life is an encounter with raw selfishness, with the need for civility, of taking turns, of being hurt and yet forgiving, and of being at the mercy of others' moods.

Family life is a constant challenge, not a periodic performance we can render on a stage and then run for the privacy of a dressing room to be alone with ourselves. The home gives us our greatest chance, however, to align our public and private behavior, to reduce the hypocrisy in our lives—to be more congruent with Christ. Home life is high adventure!

Statistics shout at us about runaway children, and the divorce rate in America now runs tauntingly near the marriage rate itself. Countless families are living in "quiet desperation," held together with the Scotch Tape of sentiment or are frozen together by the ice of indifference. The good family is the salt of society; if it loses its flavor, what will savor a tasteless society —"wherewith shall it be salted"? (See Matthew 5:13.)

This book does not try to make the case that family life will be perfect, but rather that it can be better—much better —than it now is in whichever of the three families one now lives. The book is *not* basically a how-to manual, concentrating mostly on techniques, for others have written, and sometimes well, of such things. Rather, it attempts to remind us of why we need to succeed, for our own sakes and also for the sake of other institutions. It aims at a few skills like helping and at attributes like generosity and selflessness, which are ever crucial in family life; but more often it aims at the tilt of the soul, which must precede technique.

In one survey of Church members made in 1973, the par-

3

ents surveyed reported that their greatest anxiety about adequacy in their parental roles was felt not in matters involving technique, but in the teaching of Church doctrines and from the scriptures. This anxiety appears to reflect the responsibility given to us by the Lord. Parents are reminded that the spirits that come into their homes as babes are "innocent in the beginning," and that parents in Zion have a responsibility to "bring up your children in light and truth" and are accountable to teach their children "to understand the doctrine of repentance, faith in Christ the Son of the living God, and of baptism and the gift of the Holy Ghost by the laying on of hands. . . ." (D&C 98:38, 93:40, 68:25.) Accordingly, the emphasis of this book is basically doctrinal, though some techniques are discussed.

There are no shortcuts to celestialness. But once the basic strategic commitments are made, the tactical problems are solvable. Dozens of different scriptural writers apparently have seen little point in trying to deal with technique or with interim detail, as intriguing as it might be to us now.

In a way, to ask for definitive information of a tactical character is to miss the strategic point. It was a *how* mistake that Nicodemus made after Jesus had described the importance of every individual's being born again. Nicodemus asked, logically, how a man could enter his mother's womb again. He had missed the *what* and *why* points, which we all so often have a way of doing when we are in the presence of a powerful truth. Rather than being meek and accepting, rather than pondering, we immediately want to try to fit that truth into our frail, finite framework of logic or to connect it up with our limited experience. Understandably, we desire to possess the preferred truth by shaping it to fit into the contours of our existing knowledge when what really needs to happen is that we must be overwhelmed by the truth, surrender to it, be possessed by it, rather than to be the possessors of it. We cannot make room in our little puddle of knowledge for the sea itself!

Surely that element of scale was present in Moses' realization after the panoramic vision he received when, in a great burst of both appreciation and candor, he said, "Now, for this cause I know that man is nothing, which thing I never had supposed." (Moses 1:10.)

The acceptance of things so powerful and so simple, things that we have never supposed, is often required of those who walk along the straight and narrow path.

In addition to accepting new information, we also need to ponder those things that we already know but that we need to be reminded of, because in family life we *can* do better and we *should* do better, for in a very real sense our family is mankind.

Today, while we know parts of more and more people, we also know fewer and fewer people well; our parents tended to know fewer people but these they knew more fully. Since we know so many others, either functionally or fractionally, the family, in addition to its other blessings, also gives us our best opportunity for wholeness. Not only is salvation a family affair—so are belonging and knowing!

CHAPTER TWO

Salvation is a Family Affair

*E*lder Mark E. Petersen of the Council of the Twelve has stated that "the home in a sense is like a miniature branch of the Church." The health of the Church, in many ways, is best measured in those branches, and its future is to be found there too. By his words, Elder Bruce R. McConkie reminds us that "salvation is a family affair." Indeed, Latter-day Saints do see the family in a special way. In 1902 President Joseph F. Smith said that it is "family life on which the government of the Church is based and perpetuated."

Because our family units have the possibility of being eternal, and because, meanwhile, they are the basis of the government of the Church, we have nothing more important to do than to succeed in our homes. This does not mean that we should be insensitive to our roles and activities outside of the home, but rather that the obligations that rest upon us in connection with family life are sufficiently heavy and serious that we should not lightly lay them aside for anything else.

A failure to see the importance of the family institution, a failure displayed by many today, is tantamount in some respects to the circumstances in which a people anciently "despised the words of plainness, and killed the prophets, and sought for things that they could not understand. Wherefore, because of their blindness, which blindness came by looking beyond the mark, they must needs fall." (Jacob 4:14.) So often in human affairs, individuals and groups have been guilty of "looking beyond the mark"—of looking at, or for, something that was neither a realistic hope nor a solution for their problems. Such defective farsightedness neglected the remedy that is nearer at hand all the time. It is so with Jesus' first advent. It is so with the family today, for looking beyond the family to other institutions, programs, or activities—which may be good and helpful in their spheres—can be disastrous.

The family is still the most efficient means for producing human happiness and human goodness, as well as for preparing us for the world of immortality that is to follow.

There is, for instance, fresh and justifiable concern today over the need to increase protein production to avoid famine. There is fresh and justifiable concern over developing new and clean sources of energy. In the articulated concern over these real challenges, more efficient systems are being sought. For instance, it is reported that beef cattle foraging on a fair to poor range may require twenty pounds of food in order to produce one pound of gain. On the other hand, chickens with a good balanced diet can produce one pound of gain for every two pounds of feed. The one approach is many times more efficient than the other. So, too, the human family is potentially much more efficient in producing the social and spiritual outcomes we desire than are our political, educational, economic, and other institutions. These other institutions are needed, but they cannot substitute for the home. Presently we have far too many humans "foraging" on deficient "homesteads" and too many governmental programs that attempt to substitute less efficient ways of helping humans than the family. It is the home that we must rescue and sustain. Only when homes are full of truth, trust, and love can our other institutions perform their important tasks. When too many homes become defective, then the deterioration chain-reacts contagiously and becomes inter-institutional, affecting schools and governments, for instance.

There is a veritable surf of statistics crashing all about us flowing from secular research about the importance of what happens in the early family life of individuals. Thus secular solutions that ignore the family often become not only counter-productive but also dangerous.

The tendency to worry foremost about challenges outside ourselves and our families and to look outside ourselves and our families for solutions, as well as the tendency to focus on external menaces, is too familiar to need much documentation. Perhaps an analogy out of English history will suffice insofar as misplaced hope is concerned, however.

A good friend, Dr. Jack H. Adamson, observed in a commencement speech the relevance (to modern foreign policy) of a segment of British history as follows:

> *Over three hundred years ago, a legend had grown up in England that . . . the warrior-angel, St. Michael, would appear in Cornwall if the nation faced destruction. Spain had been England's enemy for so long that an assumption had also grown up that St. Michael, when he appeared, would always look towards Spain. But time falsified that fixed idea, and Spain actually had long since ceased to be England's principal enemy; rather, the peril now was from within—from growing anger and violence, from inflated rhetoric and lack of understanding, and a young poet who knew this believed that the angel was now looking in the wrong direction. He tried to give England a new policy and he succeeded, at least in giving her a line of great poetry, when he wrote, "Look homeward, angel, now with compassion."*

For those who are inclined to look outside the family (as well as outside the individual) for solutions to challenges that either originate in the family or that can only be solved there, there is yet another great modern relevance in the lines of John Milton: we also need to "look homeward . . . now with compassion."

Only when we begin, more of the time, to look at things in terms of their impact on the family will we begin to build surely and firmly on that foundation which can sustain the social superstructure. One author made the observation, for instance, with regard to public welfare programs that "Urbanologists have been having similar qualms about the effect of welfare on the family structure—particularly in view of the alarming proportion of fatherless families. . . ." Without a clear and orthodox understanding of the doctrine of family, the casualty list of sincere but unproductive governmental efforts will grow even larger.

The beginning of wisdom is a true understanding about God, about man and the universe, for the Lord defined truth as "knowledge of things as they are, and as they were, and as they are to come." (D&C 93:24.) This marvelous insight permits us to understand yet other truths with a true perspective. Jacob wrote relatedly, ". . . for the Spirit speaketh the truth and lieth not. Wherefore, it speaketh of things as they *really* are, and of things as they *really* will be. . . plainly, for the salvation of our souls." (Jacob 4:13. Italics added.)

The presence of that powerful adverb *really* gives an emphasis to the realistic approach of the gospel. With such perspective, one sees the institution of the family in a far different light than do secularists. Surely one need not be a particularly perceptive person today in order to notice how the sonic boom of sexualism is sending sharp shudders of selfishness throughout our society, bringing other consequences that are incompatible with family life and with the calling of true parenthood. Nothing that emphasizes selfishness is ultimately compatible with the requirements of true family life or, indeed, true civilization.

It is no accident that a society that is lacking in political humility is also lacking in humility at home. It is not mere happenstance that a society like Sodom that was swamped in sexualism was also a society that neglected its poor.

When we leave off our family duties to do something of a lower priority, no matter what the immediate psychological or social gratifications of these other tasks may be, we are trading off long-term joy for short-term satisfaction, a satisfaction that may soon sour.

Lest this book sound like a special pleading for the home that is made in isolation of other considerations (because all good institutions and good causes do matter, and what is going on in the world around us matters very much), then we should ponder the wise words of columnist David S. Broder, who observed something about the positive and productive interrelationships of life on a small Beaver Island. Broder wrote: "In the small society of Beaver Island . . . family ties, assured religious faith, and a fierce . . . determination to survive impelled men and women spontaneously to clean and paint the school house, build a medical center, and put up a new dock." ("Observations 75," in *Commentary,* May 1972, p. 76.)

When, however, a society—small or large—ceases to have family ties and shared values, then the social strands that tie it together go limp.

Our larger society seems to be headed in the direction that Alexis de Tocqueville foresaw, when so many would "retire into a narrow and unenlightened selfishness."

Failures, or partial failures, of so many of our political, economic, and educational institutions spring more than we care to admit from failures in our families. Some day, perhaps before it is too late, secular research will show the correlation between the institution of the family and our relative successes and failures elsewhere in society. But the tardy making of those ties (in a scholarly way) won't really help much except perhaps for a few. Only those who start now to care about the family and who start out by believing that there are moral absolutes will have both adequate direction and motivation.

If the world's future—locally and internationally—depends in part on those who are now enemies becoming friends, and if we must strive to love our enemy, where can we obtain better experiences in giving and receiving love than in the family? Thus even our enemies finally depend on our family's capacity to have "love at home."

Edmund Burke sagely said of the interrelationship of liberty and appetite:

Men are qualified for civic liberty in the exact proportion to their disposition to put moral chains on their own appetites; in proportion as their love to justice is above their rapacity; in proportion as their soundness and sobriety of understanding is above their vanity and presumption; in proportion as they are more disposed to listen to the wise and the good in preference to the flattery of names. Society cannot exist unless a controlling power upon will and appetite be placed somewhere; and the less of it there is within, the more of it there must be without. It is ordained in the eternal constitution of things that men of intemperate minds cannot be free. Their passions forge their fetters.

Can we really speak of cultural reform without speaking first of family reform?

Those who deplore the general absence of moral content from movies and television are not mere prudes but are rightfully concerned about these two powerful forces that do so much to mold and to shape society. Duncan Williams courageously questioned a group of American professors of literature a few years back as to whether or not a "psychological poison" was destroying our minds and moral fiber.

The saturation of the western world with violence and animalism concerns not only men like Duncan Williams, but others. Indeed, it is one of the ironies of our time that the producers of sick drama and sick literature regard themselves as being highly individualistic when, in fact, they are the lemmings of literature, a conforming mass movement.

Those who understand something about what makes Satan run can appreciate the wisdom of Duncan Williams when he warns:

However, much of contemporary literature no longer supports the human spirit; if on the contrary it spreads despair, alienation, and spiritual sterility, then it is contrary to the survival of the species and should be challenged. Man is more than a physical animal. He needs, above all, hope to endure. The destruction of such hope and the dissemination of nihilism are the effects of the New Impuritanism, which . . . springs from a barely concealed cultural, social,

11

and individual death wish. (National Review, *December 21, 1973, pp. 1406, 1408.*)

A wise prophet centuries ago warned us about that nexus with nihilism, Satan, who "seeketh that all men might be miserable like unto himself." (2 Nephi 2:27.) The loving family that follows true principles is the best antidote to animalism and nihilism.

Can we talk either about education reform and not talk first about family reform?

Mary Jo Bane and Christopher Jencks have concluded that "children seem to be more influenced by what happens at home than by what happens at school." (*Saturday Review,* September 16, 1972, p. 40.) These same researchers indicate that the character of a school's output depends largely on "input," the characteristics of the entering children. Families are the source of input to our schools. James Coleman concluded, according to an article in the *Wall Street Journal* in 1966, that "home background is more important to a child's scholastic success than anything the schools have so far been able to offer."

It isn't that the schools don't make a difference; they can and do. But the differences they can make in isolation from the home are much less than has been imagined.

Governments face much the same dilemma. In a sensitive and candid memorandum, Saul Rosoff, then acting director of the Office of Child Development, advised his colleagues in the Department of Health, Education, and Welfare, in a memorandum dated April 18, 1973:

> *We also recognize that while these extra familial considerations impact heavily on child welfare, the most important force influencing the lives of children, especially the very young children, continues to be the family. . . . It is therefore critical, as we think about and plan for children's service programs, that we seek to work with and through families, not around them or without them.*

If we unwisely push onto governments the management not only of our economy, but also the management of our children and our morals, unlike Mr. Rosoff, the civil servants of the future may be neither civil nor servants!

Indeed, the health of the family is a better barometer of things to come in our political and economic world than we may care to admit. The malcontents and assassins and militants who will do so much to harm society tomorrow are already aflame in the overheated family furnaces of today. It could be said of our increasing social interdependency that never have so few been able to hurt so many so much.

Just as a giant solar flare reaching skyward from our sun ends up causing stormy weather on the earth, today's failure—or success—in an obscure family thousands of miles away may touch us later far more than we know. Dr. Dean E. Turner has written wisely: "Family love is the prism through which God's grace shines brightest into the world." For a world in need of more light and love, how precious a prism the family is!

Not only have some natural families faltered, but the quest for emancipation has also spread to surrogate parents. In recent years American universities and colleges have retreated in a headlong manner from the tradition of *in loco parentis*. It is reported that one student in an ironic outburst declaimed the retreat from *in loco parentis* with this anguished statement to assembled faculty and students: "I think you should know that that leaves a lot of us without any parents."

It apparently *doesn't* go without saying that what we learn in the home with regard to our capacity to love, to cope with change, and to be fair and genial affects us profoundly for the balance of our lives. The psychopath offers some sobering clues for us all. Of such, William and Joan McCord wrote:

> *The psychopath feels little, if any, guilt. He can commit the most appalling acts, and yet view them without remorse. The psychopath has a warped capacity for love. His emotional relationships, when they exist, are meager, fleeting, and designed to satisfy his own desires. These last two traits, guiltlessness and lovelessness, conspicuously mark the psychopath as different from other men.* (The Mask of Sanity, *St. Louis: C. V. Mosby Co., 1964, p. 450.*)

We may not personally know a psychopath, but even when the distortion of the soul is less severe than in the psychopath, we still see in some of those around us the more common consequences of inadequacy in giving and receiving love.

Much has been written about the so-called nuclear family in terms of the special challenges of our time, changing life styles, etc., and the concerns expressed by some of these writers are worthy of consideration. But one cannot help but wonder if the analogies appropriate to the nuclear family do not, in fact, also include emotional chain reactions, overheated reactors (instead of a love-at-home), and an ever-pressing sense of anxiety instead of peace.

Another researcher, Dr. Michael Craft, concluded, "The worse the parental relationship, the worse the behavior disorders seem to be." He also wrote that "from the community point of view, it is the negatively oriented parent that produces a negatively oriented child," with the child's resultant feelings arising from "parental neglect, disinterest, or hostility." (*Psychopathic Disorders,* London: Pergamon Press, Ltd., 1966.)

How much more research do we need to amass about the serious human consequences of rejecting fathers and highly indulgent mothers before we begin to deal with the need for reform, not at the level of hospitalization, but at the level of the home?

Psychopathic children have often been "raised by parents who did not want the child, who were in perpetual conflict with each other, and who violently abused their children." The results produce a human who possesses "bottomless hostilities and endless bitterness, who feels cheated in life, views himself as the victim . . . and is grossly lacking in guilt sense over his misconduct." (William and Joan McCord, *The Psychopath,* Princeton, New Jersey: D. Van Nostrand & Co., 1964.)

The McCords maintain that the failure of some individuals to develop a conscience "flows logically from the psychopath's lovelessness." Since conscience is connected not only to trust but also to love, how unconcerned can we afford to be about lovelessness? Ought we not to be concerned enough about the lyrical lament (there is never enough love to go around) to also be concerned about nurturing the locus of love: the family? Since the "internalization of moral controls takes place through the child's acceptance of his parents," according to the McCords, how unconcerned can we afford to be about parental love and values?

In a world filled with growing unchastity, and yet in which there is a growing sanction of such a swinging way of life, we should be concerned with conclusions such as those cited in a review of research on premarital sexual behavior, one of which observed that sexual relationships are also "subject to the same principles of interaction as are other relationships."

> *Relationships and their outcome seem to be governed by principles which are unvarying and cannot be repealed. . . . There is no tempering of the consequences of dishonesty, lack of self-discipline, and lack of respect for the rights of others upon interpersonal relationships . . . and no one . . . can change this fact. . . ."* (Journal of Marriage and Family, *February 1971, p. 46.*)

One is put in mind of even more insightful language, such as that in the book of Jacob, concerning another period of time when there was gross unchastity and when victims were described as living in a culture in which "many hearts died, pierced with deep wounds." (Jacob 2:35.)

Without the guides of the gospel and of living prophets, we can all be caught up into various fads and fashions having to do with child rearing. In such a situation, we can very easily slide into permissiveness. One research report observed that "in families where parents create a setting in which children exercise the power, the children tend to remain insensitive to the needs of others. . . ." (*Journal of Marriage and Family,* February 1971, p. 101.)

How important it is for children to have good adults in their lives, in addition to their parents! Yet how often our social systems today are such that "little encouragement is given to the establishment of relationships with adults outside the family." (*Journal of Marriage and the Family,* November

1970, p. 18.) How doubly tragic it is, therefore, when those relationships do not even exist *within* the family!

Long before the world began to concern itself much with such conclusions, the late President Stephen L Richards of the First Presidency asked to have fathers placed back at the head of the family: "For generations we as a Church have been endeavoring to . . . put and keep Father at the head of the family, and with all our might we have been trying to make him fit for that high and heavy responsibility." (General Conference Address, April 6, 1958.)

Now, nearly a quarter of a century later, secular research suggests, "Much of the evidence of the past decade suggests that the variability of children's behavior is more closely associated with the type of father one has than with the mother," and ". . . the instrumental role of the husband is more crucial in marital happiness than social scientists have previously believed." (*Journal of Marriage and the Family,* February 1971, p. 101.)

Even marvelous mothers cannot fully compensate for malfunctioning fathers, though, as William Law observed, just as we call our first language our mother tongue, "so we may justly call our first attitudes our mother attitudes."

Obviously children need to develop the capacity to make decisions and to have reasonable independence of parents. But to proceed headlong, and too speedily, down that particular path can produce the kind of "separatism from adults [which] may contribute to a self-centered materialistic orientation among children" in their interpersonal relationships. (Ibid., p. 102.)

However much research the world does, it still may be lacking in a central theory; it may be data-rich and theory poor. For instance, one summation of research on the family makes this very point in stating that "the field of marital therapy is in serious need of a theoretical base from which to operate." (*Journal of Marriage and the Family,* November 1970, p. 517.)

Thus, in many ways there is an urgency about restoring the family to the proper place in the priority of things. Common sense, which usually precedes research findings, tells us that we should not neglect this institution of the family.

The foregoing samples simply underscore some of those things that the prophets have said for so many centuries. Even in a church setting we need to place our priorities wisely. Elder Boyd K. Packer of the Council of the Twelve has counseled:

Presiding officers in the Church are changed from time to time, but not so with the father and mother. What happens when a father is not diligent in his responsibility? Sometimes we may even think he ought to be replaced, but who has the authority to do that? A bishop can release a Sunday School president, but he cannot release the father of a family. He has not that authority, nor has a stake president. Do the General Authorities of the Church have that authority? I know I cannot release a father from presiding over his family. His calling is special; it is permanent in the new and everlasting covenant, and no release is contemplated.

If the family really is the basis of government for the Church, if it is the seedbed of citizenship and of political leaders for the governments of nations, and if it is where we first really learn to love, to forgive, to repent, to cope with failure—*and it is!*—then we had better "look homeward"—now! For so far as the institution of the family is concerned, we neglect it at the peril not only of our present personal happiness, but of our civilization and of our salvation as well.

President John Taylor told members of the Church that "God will hold you responsible for those you *might have* saved had you done your duty." (*Journal of Discourses,* vol. 20, p. 23.) Surely that large circle of accountability includes, first, those in our family.

CHAPTER THREE

Hand to the Plough

*J*ust suppose that there is only one way for God to save men, only one path they can travel if they want to be rescued. Just suppose, too, that requirements for finding that path and staying on it are basically very simple but also very exacting. Therefore, this loving Father, who is our God, must continue to repeat these basic, simple instructions over and over again. Just suppose, also, that any variations from those recurring instructions in the scriptures result in great human misery and destruction. Just suppose, too, that this repetitive revelation of how man must negotiate the breathtaking climb on that straight and narrow path will be resented by some of the travelers on that path and will be rejected by even more individuals who refuse altogether to be directed thereunto.

In such a situation, does a loving God, who is an omniscient Father, really have any choice to do other than what he has done in his communications to us through his prophets? His messages do not cease to be relevant just because they are repeated, rejected, or resented. (A Father is not kind at all if, in an effort to be broad and nondirective, he causes us to fall off that precipitous straight and narrow path.) His message does not need to be lengthy or elaborate in order to help us take short, safe steps along that adventurous path. How very understandable, then, it is that a God who is perfect in his attributes of love and truth would decry the dangerous practices whereby men seem so repetitively insistent on a dangerous life-style in which "every man walketh in his own way"—into destruction!

So much depends on our understanding fundamental things (which are also simple things) about the nature of God, the nature of man, and the nature of ourselves. The Prophet Joseph Smith observed, "If man does not comprehend the nature of God, he cannot comprehend himself." This sunburst of celestial sense must be at least partially appreciated to provide identity and to avoid alienation, but also in order to appreciate man's true situation. For if God and man are really of two different strains, we can never really come together; even when the Savior visits this planet, it would be the visit of a stranger and an outsider. But if he is our Elder Brother, and if we are all a part of a divine family with a destiny, then, indeed, many things begin to make sense.

Is it just possible that our Heavenly Father understood the challenges of our Elder Brother, Jesus, not alone out of God's omniscience, but also in a more firsthand way?

But Jesus answered them, My Father worketh hitherto, and I work.

Therefore the Jews sought the more to kill him, because he not only had broken the sabbath, but said also that God was his Father, making himself equal with God.

Then answered Jesus and said unto them, Verily, verily, I say unto you, The Son can do nothing of himself, but what he seeth the Father do: for what things soever he doeth, these also doeth the Son likewise.

For the Father loveth the Son, and sheweth him all things that himself doeth: and he will shew him greater works than these, that ye may marvel. (John 5:17-20.)

That Divine Parent's relationship to us includes some immense possibilities!

The gospel is demanding in terms of what we are asked to believe. If we do believe, for instance, in the multiplicity of those events (what some would call the supernatural happenings) spoken of in ancient and modern scriptures, we are at once taken to a "space platform" and are admitted to a theological vista that provides a breathtaking view of the universe, of man, of history, and of the future. It is a view so overwhelming that even a glimpse tests our comprehension, especially our willingness to believe that we, individually, are a precise part of such a grand scheme. But once the core truths are accepted, we are inevitably and irretrievably set apart from the world—in order to help the world. Being so set apart, we must not be proud or condescending as we see others struggling so sincerely, for what we hear in much of the world today is the sound of real pain.

Without such a true and transcending theology, men move toward animalism and absurdity, and the sounds emanating from that sad and swelling caravan are the sounds of misery masquerading as mirth.

In his book of cartoons about World War II, Bill Mauldin had a cartoon of an old cavalry sergeant with his army pistol pointed at the hood of a disabled jeep, reflecting the tradition of the cavalryman's duty and compassion in shooting a wounded horse. Mauldin said that this cartoon was one of his favorites, but others didn't seem to appreciate all that was bound up in his repeated use of that graphic scene.

The author feels much the same way about some simple things about which he goes on writing. For instance, there are many who blithely describe the humans on this earth as the family of man but who do not believe that that family has a Father in heaven. It seems to make such individuals uncomfortable when one suggests that if we are not really the offspring of a common Father, then we are not really brothers and sisters at all. It continues to be true that the brotherhood of man is tied, inextricably, to the Fatherhood of God and vice versa. We cannot really have one without the other. Ignoring that simple fact, or making nervous jokes about it, won't do.

We are either brothers or we are not. There is either a Father in heaven who has a plan for mankind or we are unexplained transients (not brothers) in an unexplainable world who can simply make the best of things. Sometimes the most obvious things are the hardest to see and to accept.

Just as in real life, where it often takes the mediation and wisdom of a parent to bring a cessation of conflict among children, so we who live on this planet will find that our quarreling and our conflicts will not be settled finally either without the guidance of a Heavenly Parent.

Some think that it is an unacceptable admission of our own weakness to call upon God for help, but that simple, honest act is the beginning of wisdom and the acceptance of a reality which is necessary to bring peace to the noisy playground and battleground that is this planet.

Dozens of God's prophets have described to us, simply and consistently, the alternatives of righteousness and of evil, of the choices between serving the Lord and serving Satan. One possibility in explaining this leitmotiv is that in their condensation, scriptural writers were all forced to stress fundamental and basic things, but would tell us more if there simply were more space and time.

Another possible explanation for the unusual thematic rhythm in the scriptures in which fundamentals—the same fundamentals—seem to be stressed all the time is that those who come to such cosmic conclusions simply forget the intermediate points and, therefore, describe the signposts they see at the end of their spiritual journey, not those things seen at the beginning or during the journey; hence, the summational simplicity.

There is a third possibility, however, that is almost too powerful to contemplate: the writers were not short of space; they were not merely giving us an "arrived safe and well, wish you were here" message. Rather, they are telling us "of things as they *really* are." If you and I were to sit with them and converse about concepts with no constraints of time, the prophets would still stress the same simple things. What they report to be true is a repeated discovery, with every prophet so concluding and therefore stressing simple things like having faith in Jesus Christ, repenting of our sins, and choosing God and his ways. Precisely because they realize, in a very real sense, that there is no middle ground "and none other way," these prophets must tell us the same urgent basic things. This third possibility ought to haunt us!

In such a setting, the stirring words of various prophets make even more sense as they urge us to choose, to decide, and not to halt. We find, for instance, Elijah saying unto all the children of Israel, "How long halt ye between two opinions? if the Lord be God, follow him: but if Baal, then follow him." (1 Kings 18:21.)

It is too easy for us, if we're not careful, to rationalize this pleading as coming from an impatient prophet whose own ego, in a sense, was on the line, when, in fact, Elijah's message has tremendous relevancy today, for all must finally choose between the gods of this world and the God of eternity. It is an act of kindness for prophets to press mankind for a decision, because the absence of a decision to commit *is* a decision. Of course, indecision does not push us immediately into gross sin, but it renders us ineffective and uninfluential in a world that so much needs committed individuals; as a minimum, we have lost time in terms of the impact we might have had. Therefore, too much time in "no-man's land," in a sense, really puts us in the enemy's camp. One can understand, too, the prophet Joel saying, "Multitudes, multitudes in the valley of decision: for the day of the Lord is near in the valley of decision." (Joel 3:14.)

Or one can see Joshua at a time of choosing emphasizing, ". . . as for me and my house, we will serve the Lord." (Joshua 24:15.)

To have started to repent, but to have not fully repented, means that one will experience the "sorrowing of the damned." It is true of such individuals that their lives may have shed some of the gross sin, but they will still experience sorrow rather than happiness. It is the relentlessness of real repentance that makes anything but a stressing of the simple alternatives unfair to those in "no-man's land."

It would be cruel to pretend that a man who has partially extricated himself from a degree of danger (enough so that he feels some premature elation) is completely out of danger when such is not the case. So it is with men in terms of their spiritual circumstances. It is not difficult, of course, to see why the adversary would want us to be content with partial repentance, partial faith, and partial fellowship in the kingdom. He *can* settle for half a loaf, but God cannot do so and still be a god of love and truth. Of course, we will be judged by our works, and where good has been done and a certain amount of evil shunned, we will be judged accordingly. But meanwhile, while this struggle is still on, it becomes incredibly important for the disciple of Christ not to settle for merely being on the access roads or the conceptual cloverleafs that lead to the straight and narrow highway.

Part of a negative legacy of sin is that so often, even after it is given up, it can maintain a reflexive hold on an individual. It is much as if a crooked business partner is finally cast out, but the receptionist who colluded with him continues working in the office, directing and controlling the traffic to the honest partner, who somehow doesn't see that the residue of old reflexes will not permit him to take full advantage of the departure of the bad partner.

Perhaps there is even another layer of wisdom in the counsel of Joshua, when he said, "Choose you this day whom ye will serve" (Joshua 24:15), for a choice not made this day will be a difficult choice to make tomorrow, much harder next week, and very, very difficult next year.

It is also significant how many scriptures, particularly in the Book of Mormon, indicate two parts to the step of commitment: "refuse the evil and choose the good." (See 2 Nephi 17: 16.) Simply refusing the evil does not yet bring us to a point where we have in effect also chosen the good. To refuse the evil and choose the good is a two-part step: rejection and acceptance. Recall the wisdom of Mencius—it is first necessary for us to determine what we will not do, and then we can with full energy give ourselves to the things we will do. Refusing evil is an important first step, but the second step—the positive choosing of, and acting for, the good—is a necessary and vital second step, for then we stride out with a momentum that can move us further out of the reach of the adversary and into the light.

The reverse is true too; one could refuse the good without choosing the evil. Some of the harshest words of the prophets, however, are saved for those people who have chosen indifference and lukewarmness as their style. Choosing evil is also an affirmative act—no milling about uncertainly in the valley of decision; these individuals have actively chosen iniquity. Such individuals, for instance, love to lie. They prefer darkness to light. They "chose evil works rather than good." (Alma 40:13.)

Families have momentum, too, with regard to their position *vis à vis* these two powerful polarities. The most helpful thing the prophets can do is call our attention to the simple, recurring truths and the hard, unyielding requirement that we choose, for no decision is a decision that is fateful.

Families can develop negative as well as happy traditions. In some homes there develops a pattern in which some of the youth feel that it's "cool" to delay their commitment to the kingdom until after they have lived it up and acted out a kind of artificial or ritual rebellion. Those involved have no intention of going too far, or of being real rebels. They say that they know they've "got to shape up" but meanwhile, they seem determined to wait until the train starts to pull out of the station so that they must run to catch the observation car at the last moment. While we rejoice when the prodigal passenger climbs pantingly aboard the train, it is surely true that such behavior, even when it is artificial and superficial, is high-risk behavior. First of all, the time that is lost in such dalliance cannot be replaced, even when there is repentance. Second, there are some casualties; some do not really "catch the train," after all. Third, there are always other passengers in the station watching and trying to decide about their own travel plans who may question the seriousness of the prodigal passenger or the importance of the destination that he so tardily expouses.

Jesus simultaneously complimented Mary when he chided Martha by saying, "Martha, Martha, thou art careful and troubled about many things: But one thing is needful: and Mary hath chosen that good part, which shall not be taken away from her." (Luke 10:41-42.) An affirmative decision had been made by Mary within the hospitality of that home to drink in the words of the Savior, to be concerned with everlasting things. In the other case, Martha made the understandable but less significant, less wise choice, of getting supper on the table. All families must repeatedly get supper on the table, of course, but the necessary mechanics and functions of family life can drown out the good part, the memories of which shall not be taken from us. Which family style do we choose?

Indifference, indolence, and indulgence do reflect the tilt of the soul and *do* immobilize the individuals involved so far as their contribution to their fellowmen is concerned. Perhaps these are among the reasons why Christianity is so confrontive, whether it is dealing with an individual or a culture. There is kindness in that confrontation because it requires of us that we reconsider some choices that we have already made, that we be wise in the choices we have yet to make, and that we reexamine ourselves in terms of not only what we are, but what we have the power to become. There is an ideological insistence about Christianity that, at once, makes it incompatible with hedonism, or anything, that causes men to drift toward the precipice.

The gospel is not a message that will give any consolation to the wicked. It is a cutting message where there is guilt. It is a message that is hard to bear—Laman and Lemuel not only heard it but felt it so many times. There doesn't seem to have been any rebuttal on the part of Laman and Lemuel about whether or not the factual description of their shortcomings was justified. We do have indications that when they were confronted and brought up short in this manner, they were resentful—a very human reaction—but resentment is not usually a reaction that leads us to repentance. The rush of resentment tells us that we hurt, but not why. In the family of Lehi, Laman and Lemuel's resentment was heightened because the description of their deficiencies was made by someone, a younger Nephi, who was in a position to know what those shortcomings were because he could see the disturbing outlines of their lives through the added illumination that came to him from the light of the gospel of Jesus Christ. But the righteous Nephi was not practicing one-upmanship on his brothers, but spiritual statesmanship.

Deep inside the demanding doctrines of Jesus there is not only truth, but love; so also deep in the righteous reprover there is tender concern.

It is not surprising that we should squint and even shield our eyes momentarily—being in some degree in darkness—when we are first struck by the light of the gospel. The danger is that our defensive reflexes will cause us, in effect, to pull down the shade or to tell someone resentfully to put out the light. Others, when confronted by the light of the gospel, notice the presence of something special and are made visibly nervous by it, but refuse to deal with it. Such was the case with Pilate in the presence of Jesus.

A more fortunate example is the case of King Lamoni's father, who had been impressed and stirred by an illuminated individual but didn't quite understand what had happened and therefore was "troubled of mind." King Lamoni's father, however, hungered for more information and later received it humbly rather than resisting it.

True, men may "set themselves up for a light unto the world," but theirs is neon light, and it is given off by those who, for reasons other than the considerations of truth, shine to get the praise of the world.

Thus, we find ourselves always being led back to fundamentals. Nephi, having described to his brethren the importance of entering into the straight and narrow way, apparently perceived that they pondered these things in their hearts. He then reminded them that after they had received the Holy Ghost, "it will show unto you all things what ye should do." (2 Nephi 32:5.)

If his listeners, said Nephi, with reference to his words, "cannot understand them it will be because ye ask not, neither do ye knock; therefore ye are not brought into the light, but must perish in the dark." (2 Nephi 32:4.)

Once God has given us the heavenly gift, we do not need to be instructed in all details as to life at home or in the world, but we will be guided constantly by the Holy Ghost. The important thing is for us to make the basic decision to knock and to ask so that we can be brought into the light.

Far from being an intellectual dolt, therefore, the disciple who accepts the doctrines pertaining to family is unlike those knowledge-resistant souls over whom Nephi despaired, who "will not search knowledge, nor understand great knowledge, when it is given unto them in plainness, even as plain as word can be." (2 Nephi 32:7.) Some insist on continuing to play checkers when they could play chess. Some continue to hang back when they should commit.

> . . . until one is committed there is hesitancy, the chance to draw back, always ineffectiveness. Concerning all acts of initiative (and creation), there is one elementary truth, the ignorance of which kills countless ideas and splendid plans: that the moment one definitely commits oneself, then Providence moves too. All sorts of things occur to help one that would never have otherwise occurred. A whole stream of events issues from the decision, raising in one's favor all manner of unforeseen incidents and material assistance, which no man could have dreamt would have come his way. (W. H. Murray, Everest—The West Ridge, San Francisco: Thomas F. Hornbein Sierra Club, 1966, p. 100.)

Making a commitment to our Father's family and to our own family will mean that "then Providence moves too." Having put parental hands to the plow, "he that ploweth should plow in hope," for faith, hope, and charity are inextricably bound up together. The cessation of hope is a cessation of other things, too. Just as the leaning tower of Pisa is persistent rebuke to architectural pessimism, so parental hope—in refusing to topple merely because of the gravity of the situation—is a necessary repudiation of despair.

There is a reason for developing not only commitment but also capacity to spread and to defend the faith. George Macdonald warned that "it is often incapacity for defending the faith they love which turns men into persecutors." Even those, said Lehi, who have "tasted of the fruit" (the love of God) can yet fall away into forbidden paths and be lost. Why? Lehi says that some believers become "ashamed because of those" who scoff at them. Apparently the inability to defend the faith while under peer pressure may not only cost the soul of the uncertain onlooker, but the hesitant, inarticulate believer as well. No wonder Peter was desirous that believers "be ready always" to give answers to those who ask us reasons for our faith and hope. Austin Farrer counseled, "Though argument does not create conviction, . . . the lack of it destroys belief . . . what no one shows the ability to defend is quickly abandoned. Rational argument does not create unbelief, but it maintains a climate in which belief may flourish."

CHAPTER FOUR

A House of Generosity and Truth

The integrating function of family life is illustrated powerfully in that episode at Rameumptom in the Book of Mormon in which a group of people appeared on the surface to be highly religious, but among their defects, according to the prophet who described them, was this fatal flaw: "Now, after the people had all offered up thanks after this manner, they returned to their homes, never speaking of their God again until they had assembled themselves together again to the holy stand, to offer up thanks after their manner." (Alma 31:23.)

Values that are unassimilated into home life obviously fail to touch the major portion of our lives and, therefore, cannot help us either in that most important laboratory of all, the laboratory of our families. But when our homes help us to be compassionate and selfless—fundamental traits that will be touched upon later—then we have a school on whose graduates all of society depends.

Though we all may have other causes, all that we hold dear is bound up in our homes and we, too, are in the midst of a fierce battle. An ancient prophet rallied the Nephites in this manner: "Nevertheless, the Nephites were inspired by a better cause, for they were not fighting for monarchy nor power but they were fighting for their homes and their liberties, their wives and their children, and their all, yea, for their rites of worship and their church." (Alma 43:45.)

Indeed, parents in such circumstances are engaged in a bitter war and are fighting for "their all." More than we care to know, our families, our civil liberties, our religious freedoms are bound inextricably together. If one of these is peeled apart from the others, it is apt to perish. Bound together, such values can move men not only to acts of great mortal courage but, more importantly, they can move men toward heaven.

In connection with Jesus' marvelous appearance to hundreds of his disciples on the western hemisphere, we find, again, a significant reference to family and home. After he had instructed the multitude, it is significant that he then said, "Therefore, go ye unto your homes, and ponder upon the things which I have said, and ask of the Father, in my name, that ye may understand, and prepare your minds for the morrow, and I come unto you again." (3 Nephi 17:3.)

Jesus recognized the home as a place of pondering, as a place of prayer, as a place in which the men, women, and children who had heard him could get deep understanding. The above episode contains a signal contrast, indeed, to the relativism at Rameumptom, and so does this ancient counsel: "And these words . . . shall be in thine heart: And thou shalt teach them diligently unto thy children, and shalt talk of them when thou sittest in thine house, and when thou walkest by the way, and when thou liest down, and when thou risest up." (Deuteronomy 6:6-7.)

Those who flee from their neighbors and their families may say they are doing it because their neighbors (and their families) are dull, but as G.K. Chesterton observed, they are "really fleeing" because the demands of their neighbors (and their families)* are "too exciting," "too exacting" because neighbors (and families) are "alive." As Chesterton observed, we can visit Venice and regard the Venetians as only Venetians,

*Inserts in parentheses are the author's.

but the people in our own neighborhood (and in our own families) are real. We have to deal with them, not as if we were tourists, but as brothers. Our neighbors and our families are "the sample of humanity which is actually given to us." An individual in our neighborhood and in our family is a real test for our love because he is really there. Chesterton said, "It is a good thing for a man to live in a family in the same sense that it is a beautiful and delightful thing for a man to be snowed up in a street. They all force him to realize that life is not a thing from outside but a thing from inside." (*Heretics,* New York: John Lane Co., 1905.)

Because the family, in a sense, is a little kingdom containing within it great variety and many challenges, it is important to remember that when men and women "revolt against the family, [they] are, for good reasons and bad, simply revolting against mankind," since anyone who steps outside the family is stepping "into a narrower world." (Ibid.) Ironically, some individuals who cannot handle the challenge of family life so often veer off in dramatic causes to save mankind—like a drop-out from Little League demanding a place in the batting order in baseball's World Series!

Just as it is important for us to realize that God has never displayed contempt for man, though there has been sharp and justified condemnation of man's wickedness and his spiritual shortfalls, so in a family there must never be contempt for each other. Persons raised in a home where there is not contempt, even though there may be some conflict, will be much better prepared to live a life in which they see their fellowmen (though perhaps at times with irritation and disapproval) without contempt. Such individuals also will be able to see the life as having purpose and pattern—cheek by jowl with tragedy and triumph —but will never regard life with contempt.

True religion gives us both reasons and rules for life. True family life, therefore, requires true religion. In her book *Spokesmen for God,* Edith Hamilton makes the point that the Hebrews of the Old Testament—

> *were realists; they kept their eyes fixed upon life.*
> *Religion must require men to act so as not to injure*
> *one another. It must make the conditions of living*

31

better. The idea never occurred to them that it [religion] could call a man away from the world to forego marriage, comfort, pleasure, in lonely contemplation afar from the ways of common life. Religion's province was precisely the common life and the ways of ordinary men. (New York: W. W. Norton, 1949, pp. 92-93.)

Whereas the Greeks cared much for the world of ideas and were always trying to think things out, such a state of mind was unknown to the Hebrews. The Hebrews desired that truth which had a direct meaning for their lives, and could accept (in spite of life's disappointments and difficulties) truths such as the salient truth given by Isaiah: "For thus saith the Lord that created the heavens; God himself that formed the earth and made it; he hath established it, he created it not in vain, he formed it to be inhabited. . . ." (Isaiah 45:18.)

Notice how important it is that we recognize the tacit truth that lies in such a revelation about this planet and its people and its implications for human behavior. If life does indeed have purpose, and God is in command, then though life may be filled with frustrations and tragedy, one does not have to perpetually recycle doubt about himself or his place in the scheme of things. Truth does not eliminate the force of life's tragedies and frustrations, but it provides a context within which they can be coped.

Life does have purpose, and God is in his place and in command, and man is part of God's purpose, and it is in man's enlightened self-interest to cooperate in that expansive enterprise. How important it is, however, to be able to have the correct points of view about life that one can gather from the scriptures.

Learning under the direction of the Spirit of God, for instance, is much more exciting than the necessary, but sometimes bland, academic way.

No one who understands the purposes of God can, therefore, refuse to take his own responsibility for a portion of history. In such a context, little wonder that the doctrines and teachings of God matter so much. It is most unfortunate that in the surge toward secularism those who have ignored the teachings of God about the purpose of life and this planet have been so heedless; the Christian's response involves more than merely replacing the doctrinal divots on the fairway that the secularists have torn up. Even worse, as secularism has pushed out Christian thought, it has developed its own powerful dogmas it defends and, in a sense, "has turned against its own basic ideal of truth-seeking." In this regard, secularism is increasingly orthodox and is very harsh on heretics.

More than a century ago, Dostoevsky said the time would come when sages will proclaim that "there is no crime, and, therefore, no sin; there is only hunger. . . ." (Those with no absolute values would still manage to focus on appetites, however.) But the gross celebration of sensual things, the things we can feel, like thirst, hunger, and sex, can mean the destruction of so much that has been held dear.

The family is an institution inhabited by imperfect individuals, which is, nevertheless, best able to help us react sensibly and effectively to those things which imperil the family. Willie Morris wrote incisively of the so-called sexual liberation, which is so selfish that "it will ultimately begin to destroy that fragile skein of mutuality that binds men and women together," for "there has grown between lovers of my generation a fearful reluctance of any enduring mutual trust, an obsessive dwelling on the failings of the other, an urge to hurt and to tantalize—and all this buttressed and encouraged by strong and unprecedented social forces." (*Newsweek,* March 11, 1974.)

Individuals so warped could push society to a point where we are unable to conduct ourselves compassionately. One sees little generosity of spirit in Sodom and in the ugly manner in which that sensation-seeking society sought to ravish even the divine visitors.

By contrast, the king in the Book of Mormon who was deeply impressed with the generosity shown by Ammon knew that he had experienced someone who was special. This generosity can only exist in the context of selflessness. Just as fire requires oxygen, so generosity and mutuality require significant selflessness. We are accustomed to reading about the challenges of spiraling violence and spiraling inflation, and these are very real; but spiraling selfishness is at the very center of all the other spiraling challenges of today.

Because selfishness seems so much a part of the natural man, we have even built our political systems so that allowance is made for an almost automatic expression of our vested interests. But for those of us who believe in man, not alone for what he is but for what he has the power to become, it is necessary to cry out when selfishness threatens to sunder society.

Selfishness reflects a basic twisting of the structure of the soul beyond the mere instincts of self-preservation. For once an individual gives way to his appetites, a trace of momentum appears, a slight slide of the soul begins, that later can become an avalanche of appetites. This momentum can be interrupted, of course, but the more sustained it is, the more normal it seems and the less reason to resist it.

Selfishness, which comes in many costumes, is particularly cruel, not only because it gives priority to pleasure, but because it usually means one person's pleasure comes at the expense of another person's pain. Its most fundamental characteristic, however, is that one possessed of selfishness sees others as mere functions or objects to be used—or to be ignored—and not as humans to be helped, to be loved, or to be listened to. Selfishness views life in such a way that one should get all the gusto he can out of life; selfishness is the social equivalent of heedless strip-mining.

Selfishness, then, tends to encourage the view of the individual as being an assembly of appetites. Of course, sometimes we see those who are soaked in selfishness take their pleasures sadly, for there is a certain forlornness about pleasure-seeking, an artificiality to the laughter of licentiousness, and a sadness in the satiation of certain appetites temporarily satisfied.

Societies that have been unable to check spiraling selfishness are societies in which men have lost their love, one toward another, or are moved to revenge as a dominant cultural theme. The scriptures also speak of a time—perhaps ours—when the love of men would wax cold, and when men would be lovers of pleasures more than lovers of God. We are all familiar, or should be, with the scriptural portrait of those who were once believers but who became "choked" with the "pleasures of this life" and fell away. (See Luke 8:14.)

What the gospel pleads for, quite simply, is the real remedy that lies within each of us, if we are willing to be concerned with what we can do, individually, to reduce the selfishness around us. One cannot honestly say that the local application of this remedy of selflessness will change the world, but one can promise that it will change part of the world—that part which is susceptible to our influence.

One should not promise young adults that they can change the political or economic structures of the world in a summer vacation. But a summertime is sufficient time to make significant changes in each of ourselves.

Recall the scene at the Lord's Last Supper, where Jesus indicated that one of those who supped with him would betray him. Reflect on the significance of the pained inquiry in which *all* of those present ("every one of them") asked, "Lord, is it I?" One cannot diagnose and lay bare the full significance of that uniform inquiry of the Lord by the disciples, but no doubt their association with Jesus had made them much more aware of their own imperfections, so each was truly worried that it might be he. No doubt the disciples had also had enough experience with the divine discernment of Jesus to know that he could see into any recess in their souls. But clearly there was, nevertheless, a certain honesty and spontaneity about the disciples' question. They did not all look, at once, at Judas. As Kenneth L. Wilson wrote, "It is always the one who is most faithful who wonders if he is faithful enough. . . ." (*Christian Herald,* April 1974, p. 12.)

So far as meeting the challenge of selfishness is concerned, one initial temptation is to look outside ourselves to decry it in our society or to view its latest expression with alarm, because it is all around us. Rather, we must resist that temptation and ask sincerely, "Is it I?"

It is fashionable to blame systems and institutions, not individuals, for our ills, but individuals impact on our institutions—not just the other way. Whether or not we are takers or givers, therefore, does matter, for we transmit that tilt to the tasks that are ours. To warn of inordinate selfishness may be to strike a simplistic theme, and yet the immediacy and the relevancy of this theme cannot be overstated. You and I will not go to sleep tonight without having confronted specific, if only minor, situations in which we can choose either to be selfish or selfless. Who will get his car out of the crowded parking lot first? Who will wait for whom at the busy doorway out of an auditorium? Which partner in a marriage (where there may have been a few harsh words today) will be selfless enough to take the verbal initiative necessary for reconciliation? Who will put out the light? Who will get up with a crying baby? Which student will still find time to thank a particular teacher or professor who deserves to be thanked for the quality of his teaching? Indeed, the very thought process that may be going on in your mind as you read probably finds you either envisioning such specific possibilities as may lie before you this very moment or becoming rather bored by the idea of immediacy and the pending chances to be selfless. Remarkably, such specific possibilities will present themselves to you and me every day of our lives from now on.

Recall the powerful insight Jesus gave us in the parable of the unjust steward, in which the about-to-be-terminated steward makes deals with his master's debtors in order to secure his future.

Jesus contrasted therein some of the characteristics of the children of light and the children of this world. The worldly often work, realistically and energetically, "in their generation" (in their time frame), to reach their here-and-now objectives, and in that sense, as the parable concludes, they "are wiser than the children of light." Good people are sometimes too casual, too tentative, and too inconsistent in relation to eternal values.

There needs to be, therefore, a certain passion for goodness, lest, in the words of Yeats, we come to that circumstance in which "the best lack all conviction, while the worst are full of passionate intensity." Thus, those who are active, good, and selfless can constitute a counterculture, if they have a passion for their principles.

Those who are selfish are not free at all, because their only choice is to yield to their appetites. Absent absolute values, there is no good reason not to yield to appetites—*unless* there is something more important for men to do, something absolute to anchor to. It is impossible to navigate a ship, or an individual, without a point of reference, and there is no point in navigating at all if there is no destination.

Unchecked selfishness at the end of its journey takes the form of hedonism and nihilism. The distance between gross selfishness and the renunciation of self and society as being senseless is measured not in miles but inches. One Hebrew prophet, Ezekiel, described the sensual selfishness of his time as follows:

Behold, this was the iniquity of thy sister Sodom, pride, fulness of bread, and abundance of idleness was in her and in her daughters, neither did she strengthen the hand of the poor and needy. (Ezekiel 16:49.)

We must not count on sensual souls to help the poor—at least not with their very own time, money, and goods. Affluence, idleness, and lasciviousness have teamed up many times in history—and the poor always suffer.

When we stop acknowledging the existence of fixed value points in the scheme of things, we stop navigating by these points. And having stopped steering, to use a simple analogy, there is, at first, the naive, excited exclamation: "Look! No hands!" But this will be followed by the shocked realization: "Help! No brakes!" This latter condition is one of the major challenges of our society now: "No brakes!" We all seem to be expecting someone else to stop us, collectively, from doing the things we know are, historically, stupid. The specific challenges vary. For instance, the horrors of run-away inflation put us in mind of Germany several decades ago when inflated money was carried in suitcases. Surely our society has to begin to apply brakes somewhere. But to whom shall we look? Which political leaders will seriously speak and act to increase productivity or to reduce spending to help curb inflation? Alas, there are no real brakes, except those we have within ourselves.

Thomas C. Schelling has used a powerful, but simple, illustration of our society's ultimate interdependency and its reliance on cooperation, selflessness, and sacrifice. Schelling notes how cars can line up for miles on a busy highway because a mattress has fallen onto the highway; in spite of the inconvenience of hundreds of waiting motorists, each driver, once he is safely past the obstructing mattress, does not stop to remove the mattress, because now that he is past that point, the act of removal would not benefit him. The capacity to act for the good of community similarly requires us to abstain from actions that hurt others and also to inconvenience ourselves in order to help future generations. The latter capacity to anticipate, and thereby prevent, the anguish of our posterity requires the selflessness of a loving parent; it cannot be managed by those who are pleasure-seekers, for pleasure takes the form of "me" and "now," while real joy is "us" and "always."

The situation is not comical, but it brings to mind a comical circumstance. Many years ago an overweight operatic soprano was making her way through a symphony orchestra with its many music stands to her place of performance on stage. Because she was so portly, the soprano began inadvertently to knock over music stands. The excited orchestra conductor, sensing disaster, whispered to her, "Madam, please turn sideways." The soprano sadly surveyed her rounded torso and said, "Alas, I have no sideways!" In a sense, we have neither "brakes" nor "sideways."

The scriptures speak of Satan who "seeketh that all men might be miserable like unto himself." (2 Nephi 2:27.) Selfishness, run rampant, insures misery. Sensuality, carried to the end of its emotional equation, finally robs us of our capacity to feel. Selfishness in conversation, carried to its extreme, leads to verbal karate. Selfishness in a family leads not only to great conflict, but, worse, to self-hatred and self-renunciation. The acquisition of material things carried to its extreme robs us not only of our capacity to enjoy things in proper perspective, but it switches our focus from appreciation to arithmetic to mere inventory-taking.

This tendency to delight too much in acquisition was noted by Doctors Meyer Friedman and Ray H. Rosenman in their book *Type A Behavior and Your Heart*, which warns men, in particular, about a certain kind of behavior that so often precedes heart attacks:

> *This almost innate delight in acquisition probably begins quite early in our childhood. All of us have*

witnessed, for example, the delight a small boy takes in his first electric train set, even though it only consists of a locomotive and several freight cars. Later, as he experiences more birthdays and Christmases and receives more toy locomotives, freight cars, and tracks, he begins to count (rather than enjoy) the number of units he has. (New York: Alfred A. Knopf, 1974.)

Again, the obvious needs to be said, what better point or place to put the natural desire we have to acquire things in proper perspective than in our early life experiences in our families? Where can we learn better to share and to be more selfless than in our family experiences?

It was G. K. Chesterton who wisely reminded us of one of the important dimensions of real democracy: its regard for others. In our passion for the fruits and seeming decisiveness of numerical democracy, we need Chesterton's reminder not to neglect the opinions of a man even if he is our groom. Chesterton notes, too, that tradition tells us not to neglect a man's opinion, even if he is our father. Both true democracy and true religion are other-regarding. And other-regarding begins when we first encounter others—in our families.

One can only guess at the ultimate importance of those situations in the family when jousting children may be at an impasse and one child suddenly displays a "generosity of spirit" in order to bring about resolution. Experiences we have early in life in being generous, compassionate, and selfless provide a departure point for so much of what follows. Even tiny Christian acts carry with them their own satisfaction.

We can, Brigham Young observed, know that every gospel doctrine is true because it carries within itself, when it is applied, its own witness that it is true. How vital, therefore, the practicing in our homes and families of those skills and the application of those attributes which are in such short supply, such as compassion and selflessness and generosity of spirit.

Those who are grossly selfish are also the same people who, cavalierly, use ends to justify means. For the grossly selfish, once an object or desire has been fastened on, it is very easy for the selfish person to ignore the harm and injury done to others (and to institutions) when he reaches for that object. Conversely, the person who sees other men as brothers will be concerned, not alone with ends, but with means; he will understand our interdependency, and he will see others and their interests with honest concern.

Once men make of their selfish interests a religion, they tend to become very orthodox. In fact, if one reflects on the real link between selfishness and sensations, it is even easier to understand the indictment by the Savior of those who sought a sign as a condition for their belief. He describes such demands as coming from an "evil and an adulterous generation" in that they sought for a sign that they "consume it upon" their lusts. Such individuals even want theological titillation, when real religion requires us to love others, to have faith, to endure, and to be patient in affliction. Selfish individuals think of love as being only erotic and will not know the highest form of love, charity, in either the partnerships of the bedroom or in the boardrooms of the business world.

Finally, the selfish person is somewhat in the position of the drug addict; he is always in fresh need of a fix. The analogy is appropriate in other ways, in the sense that without a fresh fix, the person who is so addicted can behave injuriously and irrationally. Symptoms of withdrawal from gross selfishness are painful and, as in most illnesses, preventive medicine is the best medicine.

Selflessness requires some surgery in each of our lives; some willingness to do without, that others may have; some self-denial, that our joy in other things may be more full.

This is a matter about which each of us can do something. There are other unmet needs in the world that press in upon our minds with regard to which we are in a position of some helplessness; it would be so easy for us, however, to become focused on those distant needs to the point of being immobilized concerning the things we could do something about. Few of us have a greater chance to do lasting good in the world than in the opportunities we have within our own family every day.

There is a multiplier in the momentum of goodness (just as the reverse is true), and little cells of selflessness, such as a family, can do wonders as these cells connect up with still others who believe and behave in a similar manner.

Besides, the selfless person often gets a behavioral bonus, for it is he who will often know the joy of being able to see far enough into the hypocrite and selfish egoist to see, even there, things that are good. For the egoist and the hypocrite really hide their goodness only halfheartedly; they sense there may be goodness in their souls, but their defiance, assertiveness, and crustiness are but sentries to make certain we really search to find their goodness, for then—and only then—can they accept our report of such a discovery.

Just as life itself is not abstract but very real, so family life plays back to us, constantly, our need to be better. There is wisdom in C. S. Lewis's reminder to us all that if we want to find out if there are rats in the cellar, then fling the cellar door open suddenly. We will never see the rats in the cellar if we go tromping down the hall, giving all kinds of warnings. Family life is not alone in giving us glimpses into the cellar of self, but, more than anywhere else, we are apt to have love and understanding and specific support as we try to get rid of the "rats," for such tasks can be family projects in which we are not left alone with the task. In this same sense, Kenneth L. Wilson has written:

> *Crisis moments are revealing. They strip away carefully cultivated responses and force us to see ourselves for what we are. It is in the impulsive, unpremeditated response that we are most fully revealed. We have intended that we would do or never do this or that, then suddenly the moment is upon us, there is no time to rehearse and out of all we are and have ever been, we react.* (Christian Herald, *April 1974, p. 12.*)

Whether we make a resolution to improve in a family council or privately, sometimes sharing our resolve can give us the advantage of our pride in wanting to carry out that resolution successfully and the loving support of other members of the family. In one sense, their stake in our success is personal in that if we improve they will benefit. In another, larger sense, however, because the members of our family love us, they are sincerely anxious for us to succeed in a way that may not always be true of other associates. Even false starts and transitional failures are better understood by the members of the family. Neither will members of the family be as likely to be offended by, or scoff at, the seeming smallness of some resolution on one's part. This is so precisely because in the family life the little things are the big things.

CHAPTER FIVE

A House of Learning

*I*n view of how important it is to seek improvement in our individual lives, in our families, and in the organizations of which we are a part, it is significant that there appear to be several recurring blocks to improvement. First, there is the tendency to resist feedback or constructive suggestions. (Isn't it fortunate that Moses accepted Jethro's suggestions?) Second, there is the tendency to compartmentalize the life of an organization or an individual. Third, there is the tendency to seek early, easy answers, when what we need to do is to pray, ponder, and perspire in order to face what may be hard answers. Fourth, there is sometimes an absence of models or examples after whom a more successful pattern of living might be established. Fifth, there is the absence of divine discontent in our lives—not the restlessness of the world, but that whispering inside that lets us know we could do better and be better and that stirs us sufficiently so that we truly desire to move to a higher plane of action. Sixth, there is the presence of low self-esteem in which an individual (or an organization) thinks so little of himself that he cannot begin to rise to his potential. Seventh, there is the scourge of conceptual inadequacy, a failure to understand what one needs to know in order to do better.

Naaman, the Syrian military commander in the Old Testament, desired to be healed of his leprosy by the prophet. When he was told he had to bathe in the Jordan River seven times, he rejected that advice as being too mundane, too undramatic a ritual for someone of such lofty status as he. It is significant, however, that Naaman, when he went back to his tent, did not resist the feedback that came from his servants, who reminded him, "My father, if the prophet had bid thee do some great thing, wouldest thou not have done it?" Again the terse verse in the Old Testament tells us too little about this man or his servants, but enough for one to be full of admiration for Naaman. Having made such a public display of his rejection of the prophet's advice, Naaman did then go and bathe in the Jordan River seven times and was healed. (See 2 Kings 5.) One also has to admire the relationship and communications between this man and his servants, for his servants apparently felt free enough to speak up and make that powerful and painful observation to their chief. How often our children speak up to us as parents with parallel insights that we need to hear!

Further, when we are dealing with a block such as low self-esteem, we must remember the second great commandment, "Thou shalt love thy neighbour as thyself." Our inability to have justifiable regard for ourselves is, of course, a major block not only to our improvement, but low self-esteem is also one of the reasons why so few neighbors get loved.

One does have to be moved, however, at least to the level of desire, in order to (using Alma's words) "give place" in his life for things that need to be done. This requires at least a modest commitment, but once that trace of commitment occurs, then things begin to happen.

In view of the importance of feedback in families, here are some thoughts concerning it.

1. Positive, specific, deserved feedback is vital, does much good, and also creates a climate in which the occasional, negative feedback that needs to be given can be given and is more likely to be received. The late Supreme Court Justice Felix Frankfurter noted the need we have to face the truth even when it is pleasant.

2. We should not give feedback or be candid merely to punish or to meet our own ego needs. Rather, we must do as Paul says, speak "the truth in love," and where we must give reproof, we must do as Paul also suggested, "confirm your love" (some visible act or expression) lest the other individual "be swallowed up with overmuch sorrow." (See 2 Corinthians 2.) In the Doctrine and Covenants, we are asked to show forth an "increase of love"—*not the same level of love,* but a visible and measurable "increase." (To "confirm" and to "increase" our love are vital acts.)

3. We need to take into account the capacity of ourselves and the other individuals involved in any situation or circumstance to manage the consequence of candor. There are simply times when the risks of candor are unacceptably high; the biting of the tongue, on occasion, can prevent the tearing of a heart.

4. We should consider the appropriateness of the setting, as well as the appropriateness of what is said.

5. The feedback given should bear reasonable relationship to the importance of the issue, lest there be overkill because of mere trivia. Emotional escalation in family conflict —and elsewhere—is so often all out of proportion to the issue involved. (Big people are simply less irritated by little things.)

6. Feedback is facilitated when there is an advance and shared expectation that it will be given and is to be expected.

7. Interim feedback has the advantage of still allowing for course corrections without being so ultimate and final. It is noteworthy, in Jesus' relationship with Peter, how the Master's love was felt by Peter and how Peter grew with the mixture of love and occasional reproof.

In Proverbs 15:32 we read, "He that refuseth instruction despiseth his own soul: but he that heareth reproof getteth understanding."

Much of the understanding we can get from life can flow from deserved reproof. Of course, reproof-giving should not be a life style, but we should be able to forgive the communicator while receiving these kinds of vital communications, because they *can* be for the welfare of our soul.

Jesus counseled us, in Matthew 18:15, "Moreover if thy brother shall trespass against thee, go and tell him his fault between thee and him alone: if he shall hear thee, thou hast gained thy brother." The hearing of reproof is, of course, difficult at times. Even more difficult is the taking of the initiative in situations where one does need to "go and tell" in quiet courage.

One of the most moving episodes in all of scripture is the one in which there is a conversation between Samuel and Eli. (See 1 Samuel 3:12-21.) In this situation Samuel was given insights that pertain to Eli. Samuel, with understandable trepidation, apparently lay awake until morning, fearing to tell Eli what he had been shown. But Eli "called Samuel, and said, Samuel, my son. And he answered, Here am I." Eli asked, "What is the thing that the Lord hath said unto thee? I pray thee hide it not from me: God do so to thee, and more also, if thou hide any thing from me of all the things that he said unto thee."

Then, in this marvelous exchange, we read, "And Samuel told him every whit, and hid nothing from him. And he said, It is the Lord: let him do what seemeth him good."

That Samuel finally had the courage to do that kind of sharing, in an appropriate way and in an appropriate circumstance, was no doubt reflective of some of the same qualities in Samuel in his earlier and better years, when "the Lord was with him." In those days Samuel spoke in such a manner that the Lord "did let none of his words fall to the ground," and everyone "from Dan even to Beersheba knew that Samuel was established to be a prophet of the Lord."

One of our most constant challenges in family life and elsewhere is the challenge of helping in a way that is lastingly effective. What follows is a brief exercise that, in appropriate circumstances, can help us to focus on those particular challenges of helping which seem to give us the most difficulty.

Some of the specific and typical blocks that get in the way of our being effective helpers in our families, Church assign-

ments, *civic roles, and vocations are* (*select two that are most descriptive of your particular, recurring challenges when in helping relationships, or* [*under "Q"*] *add your equally specific challenges not listed here*):

_____**A.** I don't really delegate completely, but tend to hold onto the task myself or to take over later, not really trusting others to use their free agency, or being impatient for results.

_____**B.** I have a tendency to overrespond and to oversupply, to give more help than is wanted, such as when helping my children.

_____**C.** I have a tendency to abandon others once an assignment is made without providing on-going help and support.

_____**D.** I have a tendency to undersupply information, so that others may not really understand the implications of what they are getting into.

_____**E.** I have a tendency not to be adequately candid, finding it difficult to level with others about their performance.

_____**F.** I have a tendency to want to keep others at arms' length for fear of becoming too involved should I try to help.

_____**G.** I have a tendency to fail to set realistic limits on what kind of help others can expect from me.

_____**H.** I have a tendency to check up too little on others and their progress.

_____**I.** I have a tendency to check up too much on those I am trying to help.

_____**J.** I have a tendency to do a superficial analysis of the problem to be solved or the job to be done, leaving this task to others.

_____**K.** I have a tendency to practice benevolent manipulation.

_____**L.** I have a tendency to be too hurried, failing to set aside enough time to help.

_____**M.** I don't seem to know how to be seen as an approachable resource for others, so I feel under-used.

_____**N.** Sometimes I don't really care deeply enough about the task or the people involved to be committed to helping.

_____**O.** I have a tendency to assume that my expectations are shared and matched, only to find later the assumptions were at least partially in error.

_____**P.** I have a tendency not to listen carefully.

_____**Q.** Other (please specify). _____

This exercise is not for fun or merely to encourage superficial diagnosis. It involves one's genuine willingness to commit to specific improvement after appropriate reflecting, discussing, and pondering of the matter and by then selecting certain goals that can be worked on *now!*

Commitment portion of the exercise on helping:

1. Of the two challenges I selected involving helping, I will now focus on just one of these: _____

2. In seeking to meet this specific challenge, the most helpful principle or idea I need to use is: _____

3. In seeking to meet this specific challenge, one thing I will *stop* doing is: _____

4. In seeking to meet this specific challenge, one thing I will *start* doing is: _____

5. To help me carry out these specific commitments, two sources of unused (or under-used) help I could better utilize are:

(a) _____

(b) _____

Often we get clues from the distilled wisdom of those whom we admire. What follows are some simple efforts to reach that very objective: to draw upon the lives of significant individuals in search of some of the specific qualities they noted in their special parents that for the following individuals have had great significance. *Note, too, how the parental attributes reappear in these special children.*

President Spencer W. Kimball has vivid and specific memories of the influence of his parents, particularly of his father:

> *My mother died when I was still a child; therefore, I was not quite so conscious of her presence and her influence on me as I was my father.*
>
> *I remember many times when my father would show his special interest in me. He was the stake president. As he visited the wards of the stake, which ranged from local to 100 miles away, he frequently took me with him, and here was a good experience to get acquainted with him.*
>
> *When I was ten years old, my father took me to Salt Lake City from Thatcher, Arizona, and this was a great eye-opener. At that time there was no short-line railroad between Salt Lake and Los Angeles, so we traveled to Los Angeles and then to San Francisco and then across Nevada to Salt Lake. He took me many places in Salt Lake City and introduced me to his numerous brothers and sisters and other relatives. When we went home by way of San Francisco, we went to the pleasure park where he took me on most of the concessions and gave me many of the thrills of my life.*
>
> *He taught me another lesson as I saw his kindness and tenderness to his second wife, my stepmother, who was ill for a long time and needed a great deal of sympathy and tenderness.*
>
> *My father taught me dependability and hard work and kindness to people. He was generally up at five o'clock in the morning working in the yard, which was the prettiest yard in town and had the most flowers and the greatest variety of trees and fruits. He was an example to all his people.*
>
> *Father assigned to me this large yard, and as I grew up it was my duty to prune the trees and to cut the lawn and to hoe the weeds, and it often seemed a*

very great task, but it was excellent experience for me. He never shielded me from hard work, but I received many dividends by having done it. When I was a small boy, he bought me a small pitchfork so that I could go into the field with my older brothers and do my part.

Many times I saw him stop loading hay in the field when people came with their troubles, and he stood in the shade of a tree and counseled with them while we boys went on to pile on the hay. People came to him at all hours of the day and night for counseling, and he seemed to never be too busy to stop in the middle of any work to help them with their problems.

My father taught me reverence for holy things and to uphold and sustain leadership. He taught me many things—to love, to be kind and considerate, to help and assist, to be sympathetic, to love neighbors and friends and relatives and to make myself available always to do good.

President N. Eldon Tanner makes these interesting and significant observations about his early family life with "goodly parents":

I was born of goodly parents who loved their children, loved the Lord, and were an example of righteous living. We were taught to pray in all sincerity to a living and loving Father in heaven, realizing we were his spirit children and he stood ready to answer our call.

Morning and evening family prayer was a daily uplifting experience. I was greatly influenced by the way my father literally talked to the Lord, which helped me to understand the nature of God and that he was truly a living Being to whom I could go and with whom I could converse.

Mother always reminded me that the Lord knew what I was doing and that I should prepare myself to be worthy of some day meeting the Savior face to face.

Integrity and dependability were emphasized and taught to us by example as well as by precept. How fortunate to be one whose parents were determined to live so as to enjoy the family unit throughout eternity.

President Marion G. Romney makes this observation about his father:

Two of the great virtues possessed by my father, George S. Romney, were impeccable integrity and an insatiable desire for an education. The following incidents are characteristic of his integrity.

At the age of twenty-five when he returned from a two-year mission, Father signed the attendance roll as did others in a Mutual Improvement Association class. After the meeting the superintendent of the YMMIA, Guy C. Wilson, said to him, "Brother Romney, I hope you will be regular in your attendance." Father merely replied, "I put my name on the roll."

Years later Brother Wilson told me that thereafter Father never missed a class without a justifiable excuse.

President Romney also tells of how indelibly impressed he was in the midst of economic hardships with his father's commitment to the principle of tithing.

In 1912 Father's family, with the other war refugees from the Mormon colonies in northern Chihuahua, fled into the United States. Two years later he and his brother Gaskell, with their families—Father with eight children, his brother with six—settled in Oakley, Idaho.

Father was employed as a teacher in the Cassia Stake Academy at a salary of $80 a month. The two brothers pooled their earnings and divided their income equally.

During the winter of 1913-14, my uncle, a carpenter, could find no employment and therefore had no income. Father's salary of $80 a month had to be

*divided between the families. If tithing was to be
paid, each family would have $36 a month. If it was
not paid, each family would have $40.*

*A family council was held to decide whether to pay
tithing. The decision was to pay. For me, then 16
years of age, this was a crucial decision; I thought
it was unrealistic. How could our family, ten people,
live on $36 a month—$3.60 each? We had to pay rent
and buy fuel. Having left a warm climate and come
to a cold one, we were in desperate need of clothing.
I was sensitive and embarrassed by the appearance
of the cast-off clothing we wore. Notwithstanding
my feelings, tithing—the debt owed to the Lord—was
paid and we survived the winter. Father's integrity
paid off. He never compromised in dealing with men
or the Lord.*

Of his mother, President Romney says:

*My mother, Artemesia Redd Romney, was not a whit
inferior to my father in industry, courage, and nobility. Through all her struggles she was an uncom-
plaining helpmate and supporter. She bore him ten
children—eight daughters and two sons. She cared
for them, taught them, and raised them all to maturity with unfailing love and great faith and wisdom.*

*Although she never went to school beyond the eighth
grade until after she was left a widow at the age of
61, she was well read in literature and an artist of
note in her own right.*

Elder Gordon B. Hinckley notes that the home in which
he grew up was one in which the gospel was lived. In that
special home, Elder Hinckley recalls,

*I never heard my father speak critically of anyone.
He frequently said, "Cynics do not contribute; skep-
tics do not create; doubters do not achieve." He was
positive in his thinking but mild in his manner. Family prayer, both morning and evening, was the cus-
tom of the day; and home night, as it was called then,
was faithfully observed each Monday evening.*

We had in our home one large room called the library with more than a thousand volumes and a sturdy table at which we studied. It was the kind of atmosphere that encouraged reading. My mother complemented this with her personality and background. She had been a teacher of English and unfailingly used correct grammar. Whatever culture her children may have acquired came of her influence.

Wise parents can provide superb learning experiences in the simplest of ways. Note this vivid recollection from Elder Thomas S. Monson about his experience in Christian service during his childhood:

When the Great Depression brought to a standstill the wheels of economic progress throughout America and indeed the world, I was but a boy. My father was a skilled craftsman, hence, our family did not suffer so much as did some where the dreaded specter of unemployment visited. There were days when elderly pensioners received no financial benefits and frequently found it difficult to obtain food and shelter.

Down the street on which I lived was a small adobe home which my grandfather provided without charge to an elderly and indigent widower named Robert Dick. We all knew him as "Old Bob."

Frequently throughout the week, and always on Sunday, Mother, when filling the dinner plate of each member of the family, would prepare an extra plate and would ask me or one of my brothers or sisters to serve as messenger in carrying the delicious meal to Old Bob. When my turn came, I always ran fast, for inevitably I would be hungry and anxious to return to my own meal.

In retrospect, as I look backward to years long gone by, I remember yet the glistening eyes of Old Bob and his gracious "thank you" as the dinner was placed on a crudely fashioned wooden table and he sat down to his only meal of the day.

*I am grateful that my mother provided for each of us
this spiritual and faith-building experience, which
truly taught us to love our neighbors as ourselves.*

Elder Marvin J. Ashton recalls his father, Bishop Marvin
O. Ashton, first counselor in the Presiding Bishopric, as follows: "As I look back on significant association and impression
influences with my father, I am impressed with his powerful
example. He set up crisp guidelines and then conducted himself ably within the framework to leave no doubt as to what
he had in mind." Here are but seven of these guidelines:

1. "Keep your chin up." Don't get down on yourself or
others. Be optimistic. Don't give up.

2. "Put some water in the soup." Share with others in
their needs, even if you have to thin down your own soup to
do it.

3. "Let's speak the English language." Get to the point.
Be frank and pointed in your conversation and opinions.

4. "Measure your words and let them be few." Good
listeners are at a premium. Don't talk just to be talking or get
attention. When you speak, have something to say.

5. "Remember who you are." Conduct yourself accordingly.

6. "The world will love you if you're human." Have empathy for all you meet. Be a friend to the troubled and weary.

7. "Thank you." We are all inclined to take too little time
to express gratitude to our associates and God.

Elder Bruce R. McConkie of the Council of the Twelve,
in reflecting on his parents, shares these interesting insights:

*Everything in my parents' home was gospel-centered,
gospel-oriented, gospel-governed. Day in and day out
we talked about the principles of the gospel—not in
a speculative way, not dwelling upon the mysteries,
not considering hidden and unrevealed matters that
have little bearing upon gaining salvation. Rather,
we pondered in our hearts the basic and fundamental
things that men must believe and to which they must
conform to gain eternal life. We rejoiced continually
in the words of eternal life, hoping thereby to become*

inheritors in due course of that greatest of all the gifts of God.

Our standard family exhortation, given by parents and children alike whenever any member left the hearthside either for a long or a short period, was the familiar: Remember who you are, and act accordingly.

As McConkie children we knew we were to live in harmony with the standards of the family. As children of Him who is eternal and who had bought us with His blood, we knew we were to conform to gospel standards.

How grateful I am that we were taught by precept and example in a gospel-centered, gospel-oriented, and gospel-governed family!

Frances Grant Bennett, wife of Utah's distinguished Senator Wallace F. Bennett, recalls life in the home of her father, President Heber J. Grant: "In matters of small importance, Father seldom said no to us. Consequently, when he did say no, we knew he meant it. His training allowed us to make our own decisions whenever possible. He was able somehow to motivate us to *want* to do the right thing rather than be *forced* to do it."

Dr. Henry Eyring, internationally acclaimed scientist and brother of Sister Spencer W. Kimball, makes this important comment concerning his mother, Caroline Romney Eyring: "It was impossible for my mother to be either idle or pessimistic. Each of her eight living children had the feeling that they were special to her. They all did well in school and she never failed to praise them for it. Her selflessness made us all anxious to pull our own weight."

Dr. Eyring said, of his mother's desire that he "be good for something," that "a lifetime of effort is still too little payment to an optimistic, selfless mother."

Of his father, Dr. Eyring notes: "If he ever worried, I never knew it. To me he always seemed gracious, courageous, and wise." As a young man leaving in 1919 for the University of Arizona, he heard his father say, "Henry, I am convinced that the Lord used the Prophet Joseph Smith to restore his church, but there are a lot of other matters I don't know the answer to. Go to the University of Arizona and learn all you can. The gospel is whatever is true."

In his "underselling way," says Dr. Eyring, "my father's characterization of membership in the Church as a commitment to decency and to the truth put it on a level that was very hard to disagree with." Under such counsel, young Henry Eyring began an unusual adventure with truth and learning.

The daughter of President and Sister Harold B. Lee, Helen Lee Goates, comments about her special parents and home life with these articulate remembrances:

> *I had the ideal combination of parents: a father who was gentle beneath his firmness, and a mother who was firm beneath her gentleness. They worked at rearing their two daughters as a team, equally yoked.*
>
> *Mother believed always that a home should be an oasis in a world starved for spiritual nourishment, and therefore maintained a home of tranquillity, peace, and order, where the gospel teachings of a wise father could take root and grow in our lives. In this climate, we were shown by example how to find our answers to the complexities of life, as we moved through the daily experiences of growing up. Consistently we were taught to turn to those sacred books of scripture on our shelves when a discussion from a Sunday School class or preparation for a two-and-a-half-minute talk brought forth a question to be answered. We were instructed, "Get out your scriptures, girls, and let's see what the Lord says about it." We learned early that the intellectual, academic, philosophical answers were sought only after the spiritual essence of the matter was clearly felt and understood.*
>
> *How carefully they nurtured our tender feelings about ourselves! When the early years of striving to master musical instruments brought discouragement*

and possible failure into view, we were reinforced regularly by the positive, firm assurance that our Daddy and Mother thought we made the most beautiful music this side of heaven. When those awkward adolescent years were upon us, with their insecurities and daily threats to self-esteem, we were constantly reminded that Mother and Daddy loved us and that they were convinced that we were the loveliest, most charming young women they had ever seen. Wise parents that they were, they must have known that if they placed those images before us, we would strive to be what they wanted us to be, and what they knew we could become.

In an atmosphere of love and peace, I learned to know and to love the Lord and his holy words, and to recognize his supremacy in my life. On this firm foundation was built an appreciation and acceptance of self, so essential a stepping stone to learning the more important and mature concept of loving and serving others, which quite naturally followed.

It is very significant to see the pattern of attributes in the foregoing examples. These special parents are remembered for their simple and specific qualities, such as their optimism, their praise of children, their lack of anxiety, their poise under pressure, their understatement, their personalized prayers, their integrity, their example, their faithfulness under stress, their generosity, their teaching the gospel constantly, their love of the gospel, their lack of verbosity—the simple but profound qualities all parents need to succeed.

It is also interesting how often in these situations the parents have, in one way or another, followed much the same pattern in helping these, their children, as did the Lord in assisting the Brother of Jared in that memorable "case study" recounted in chapters two and three of the book of Ether. This episode, while it would not apply to all situations, was the best way the Lord could help the Brother of Jared in that circumstance. Implicit in it are a number of lessons for each of us, as parents as well as human beings.

1. The Lord gave the Brother of Jared an assignment. (Ether 2:16.)

2. In the course of that assignment the Brother of Jared encountered a vexing problem—the need for light in the barges (2:22)—and asked the Lord for help.

3. The Lord asked how he could help the Brother of Jared. (2:23.)

4. The Lord helped the Brother of Jared focus on the realities and alternatives. (2:23-25.)

5. The Lord left the problem and responsibility clearly with the Brother of Jared. (2:25.)

6. The Brother of Jared worked out his own problem, pursuing a specific, prospective solution. (3:1.)

7. The Brother of Jared, having done what he could do, asked for specific help from the Lord. (3:2-4.)

8. The Lord responded specifically to the request for help by providing light but utilizing the solution proposed by the Brother of Jared. (3:6.)

9. The Lord commended and honored the Brother of Jared. (3:9, 12.)

The key is often the kind of help we offer.

When a parent's teaching and helping job is done well and when there are receptive children to receive the message, then we encounter those marvelous situations such as the one involving young men in the Book of Mormon who had been taught so well by their mothers "that if they did not doubt, God would deliver them." These young men said, "We do not doubt our mothers knew it." (Alma 56:47-48.) Secondary faith is often adequate. Note the "gift" spoken of by the Lord in verse 14:

> *To some it is given by the Holy Ghost to know that Jesus Christ is the Son of God, and that he was crucified for the sins of the world.*

> *To others it is given to believe on their words, that they also might have eternal life if they continue faithful. (D&C 46:13-14.)*

The reliance, of course, by these young men on their mothers is touching and profound, but the mothers first had to know "it" in such a way that the young men, observing them closely and hearing them (as is always the case with children observing parents), did "not doubt" that their mothers knew that "it" was true. William Law observed tellingly that "it may be found more easy to forget our [first] language than to part with those attitudes which we learned in the nursery."

Dr. Neil J. Flinders of the Department of Seminaries and Institutes has pointed out how almost too much attention has been focused in recent years on the rearing of children in their adolescent years, from 12 to 18. Perhaps this is because of the excitement, vocalness, and turmoil, etc., that often go with this age period (which attracts more attention and produces more parental anxiety), that parents are, when their children are ages 8-12, guilty of "looking beyond the mark."

Dr. Flinders points out, however, that parents "have been prone to relax from the intense care of infancy and more or less rest during this relatively maintenance-free period of 8-12 years before the storm of adolescent independence descends upon them." He is "inclined to think we have not made the best use of this period in our religious educational efforts," referring to "the quiet years of 8 to 12." Often more real learning can occur during the "quiet years" than later on, when there are so many distractions and competing forces. Regardless of the children's ages, however, parental communications are crucial.

The exercise that follows is a simple one having to do with the importance of establishing two-way communication between individuals, including communications within families.* The first part involves a simple, one-way communication approach, the one that we use so often allegedly to save time, when we think that mere telling is teaching.

---

*Efforts to identify the originator of these exercises have failed, but appreciation in lieu of acknowledgment is hereby expressed for a simple but pointed contribution to communication.

One-way Two-way Communication Exercise
Part I

1. Choose a person from your family or group at random. Have this person move out of eyesight, but within talking distance, or sit with his back to the rest of the group and explain with words only (no gestures, etc.) how to draw the Diagram No. 1. (Make sure group members cannot see the model diagram.)

2. The rest of the group must be silent and cannot ask questions.

3. Only 3 minutes can be given to the person to explain the figure and for the group for this attempt to reproduce the diagram.

4. When the 3 minutes are up, stop.

Diagram No. 1

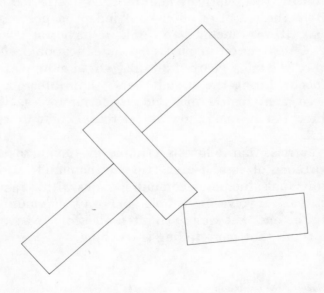

Part II

5. Keep the same person up front, but now give him Diagram No. 2 with the same objective, but according to these new rules:

    a.   The group can see the describer and ask him questions about the instructions he gives.

    b.   The describer cannot show the diagram but he can watch participants' reactions and use gestures.

    c.   Take 3 minutes for the task and then stop.

6. Have the group compare the accuracy of their diagrams No. 1 and No. 2 (shape, size, angles, etc.) with the models.

7. Have the group talk briefly about their experiences in terms of frustrations, key break-throughs in communication, the relative efficiencies of one-way and two-way communication.

8. If a family is involved, have brief discussion as to the implications of the exercise for family life.

Diagram No. 2

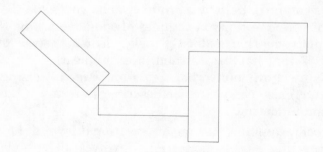

Typical Observations About
The One-way Two-way Communication Exercise

(Note: It is better if most of the observations come from the family or group, but one or two of the observations below might be used as a "primer" or to supplement what the group offers by way of observations.)

1. The describer probably feels he was doing an accurate job of describing Diagram No. 1 and probably felt the frustration that leaders sometimes feel when they give instructions, but followers don't seem to get the message. This often happens in family and church situations.

2. Sometimes a one-way communicator unintentionally puts off his listeners by being too imprecise, using wrong words, or being too technical.

3. Note how two-way communication freed the group to ask questions, to clarify statements by the describer as to size, shape, angles, etc.

4. Note how one good question can often clarify for others who had the same question but who may have been hesitant to ask it.

5. Note how two-way communication is usually not only more efficient, but can also save time in the long run.

6. Note how two-way communication gives us feedback as to how well instructions are coming across.

7. Note how important being able to ask key clarifying questions can be in helping a group to achieve its goals. (There will usually be one or two examples of someone asking the describer questions that suddenly make clear an aspect of Diagram No. 2 that had, up to then, been unclear.)

8. Note how nonverbal reactions (facial expressions, posture, etc.) also can guide the describer in terms of how well he is communicating.

A good example at a nonconversational level of how one-way instructing has its limitations involves an episode from the author's own family. When our daughter Becky was about eight, she was asked by her mother to run home between Sunday School and fast meeting and stick a fork in each potato that was baking in the oven, since baking potatoes sometimes explode. When we all got home and Colleen opened the oven door, there were six forks—one standing erectly in *each* of six potatoes! Becky had followed instructions carefully and literally, as we so often do when there is only one-way communication and with no chance to ask clarifying questions about intent.

Even when parents are in a helping relationship with their children, we can learn so much from them too. Insofar, however, as we are often in a helping relationship, it may be useful for us occasionally to take an inventory of how helpful we really are.

For instance, the author's 17-year-old daughter, Nancy, several months ago needed a little help on a question involving an important case (*Fletcher* v. *Peck*), decided by the United States Supreme Court early in its history. As a father who is so inept when called upon to help with subjects like algebra, at last this seemed like a glorious invitation. Quickly and enthusiastically, I confronted my daughter with an array of books dealing with the Supreme Court case. I even found some of my old political science lecture notes. Then I paused long enough to notice the look of dismay on Nancy's face. She didn't want *that* much help; I was extending to her more help than she needed. After all, she only needed a single paragraph, and I had virtually swamped her with excess help. On that occasion, my need to give help outran her need for help.

For those of us who have over-helped someone else, this simple story may be a useful reminder. We should size our responses to match the requests we get for help.

On another occasion I was somewhat more helpful. Our teenage son, Cory, came home obviously upset; he had just had a brief fist fight with a best friend. He told me anxiously what had happened and was obviously sick at heart and expecting parental reproof. I remember acknowledging the sincerity of his regret with a simple, sincere sentence or two, seeking to put the episode in perspective, and then, naively, being surprised to see the immense relief pass over his face. He had already condemned himself enough; he expected but got no condemnation from an adult "court."

Our thoughtful daughter Jane, at age three, returned from play at a neighbor's house and Colleen asked her, "Were you a good girl?" Jane said, "No." Her mother asked, "Were you a bad girl?" Jane said, "No." "What were you then?" Jane replied, honestly, "Just medium." This sweet episode on which our family has reminisced is a sobering reminder that our children usually know pretty well how they are doing. They certainly don't want to be neglected when they are good, for they deserve and need wise praise. But neither do they wish to be praised undeservingly. Most of us know how we are doing and when we are just "medium." Too much superficial sentiment from parents may create a mesh of disallowance through which the honestly deserved compliment has difficulty passing.

Of course, we transmit our feelings to our children in many ways. For those of us who do not have poker faces and whose emotions seem to register fully and immediately, this story may press the point better than a theoretical description of the importance of nonverbal communication.

Our family was privileged to go to Europe together several years ago. The author tends to be over-organized and often plans too precisely, and then suffers double disappointment when plans go awry. My wife and children saw several times on that trip what came to be known as my "Europe face." This pained expression was visible on those occasions of tourist irony when the best-laid plans came apart, or when some surprising development occurred, such as the unexplained cancelling of our needed hotel reservations. On such occasions the look on my face said, "You're kidding! This isn't really happening, is it?" For instance, the "Europe face" appeared when I hustled our family off one side of a stopping train. We saw, too late, that we had gotten off the wrong side of that long train (bags and all), and that we would not be able to get on the other side of it quickly enough to catch the waiting express train, which pulled out without us a few minutes later. My family was more amused than distressed, for there would be other trains, and this helped to give me some needed kidding about my sense of time urgency.

Our children see us insightfully in other ways too, when, for instance, we chronically violate some less weighty standard of behavior. It suggests to them that we are not fully serious about the gospel standards. Unfortunately, not only do they sometimes see us as unserious about *that* particular principle or standard, but they may think we are less serious than we really are about other standards. In any event, if our children may later take unjustified license and feel it's all right to cut corners, they may pick their own corners to cut when they grow up, and the corners they choose to cut may be far more serious. This wisdom first came to my attention from the late and wise Oscar W. McConkie.

We had a kind of "exit interview" with our oldest daughter, allowing for some feedback to us as parents, as she prepared to marry in the temple a few days later. We gave her, in a family home evening, a chance to reflect upon us as parents. She was gentle and kind but managed to observe that on one occasion she deeply, and particularly, appreciated being trusted by us. Apparently that situation meant much more to her than we realized then, though we were aware that it was an important circumstance. We had cause for parental anxiety about the circumstance she would encounter but, fortunately, tipped the scales toward trust. How often a moment is crucial for one person and yet is not so regarded by another. Perhaps one of the simple things we could do more of in family life is to level with each other about when something really matters—as long as we don't cry "wolf" too often! So much depends, therefore, on how we communicate.

Our homes are places in which we may talk about the need for us to become perfect even as our Father in heaven is perfect, and about the principle of eternal progress.

Does, however, our home reflect a serious commitment on the part of the parents, as well as the children, to find better ways of doing the simple, daily things? We're not talking here about the doctrines of the Church (which are perfect and which cannot be improved upon), but simply about duties and a life style of the family. Are we really open to improved ways of doing mundane things, like the chores? Sometimes the mere presence of a suggestion-box climate in a home, as opposed to parental rigidity about how, for instance, chores should be done, is more vital than we know. Parental openness to better ways of doing mundane things can increase our children's respect for us in weightier matters where, in fact, parents usually do know what is best.

Too often, too, our children are underwhelmed in terms of responsibility and the things we give them to do. It strikes the author as strange that some of us should miss something that is so on-goingly obvious in the Church: the period of the most remarkable growth and maturation for many young adults in the Church is usually the period when they are serving as full-time missionaries. Isn't it interesting that among the ingredients of this experience are learning conditions in which (1) we give to these young adults significant and specific responsibilities; (2) we trust them, but do not abandon them in terms of supervision and evaluation; (3) we treat them like adults and most of them become adults; and (4) they almost always get a witness for themselves that the Church and gospel are true, for the Holy Ghost tells them so. (Parenthetically and ironically, so often when these maturing men and women return from their missions we proceed to underwhelm them once again.)

We can underwhelm our youth. Indeed, the present protracted period of education in America may lie at the heart of many of our intergenerational problems. Our children are too often not only passive spectators in classrooms, but they end up in the same role of repose at home or in a neighborhood. So many make-work service projects are but a sobering reminder of how far removed some youth now are (not by their choice) from the world of work.

It may take more imagination and commitment to give the relevant things to our youth to do in the world of work but, in fact, these are among the very links with reality that are so desperately needed by so many of our children and our youth.

There is something about appropriate authenticity that is deeply conducive to lasting learning.

When either our methods of teaching or our objectives are too contrived, the learner usually perceives this defect. In the same way, parental behavior that is superficial is usually an ineffective teacher. Parental behavior that is not sustained will seldom impress or teach.

Too often, we fail to see the connection between family experience and the leadership styles we carry into our church service. Just as we can flit unsuccessfully from objective to objective in our family, so it becomes easier later on in a church assignment to flit from unachieved goal to unachieved goal, from emphasis on one program to emphasis on yet another program. In such situations it ought to be clear that sometimes it is not our goal that needs changing, but our level of effectiveness.

It is ordained that our trials and our experiences in life must be real and must be authentic, not abstract. There can't be any game playing or play acting, for we would be quick to see that. The agony, the growth, the testing, and the joy must be real—real enough that they call forth in us the things that can only be mobilized under such conditions. And these realities start being felt first in the family.

It should not surprise us that great men like John the Baptist, after reposing in a jail, wondered whether he had been forgotten and whether or not He for whom he had prepared the way was really Jesus after all.

It shouldn't surprise us that the agony on the cross was so real that even the Very Best cried out, wondering if he had been forsaken.

Moroni cautioned, ". . . dispute not because ye see not, for ye receive no witness until after the trial of your faith." (Ether 12:6.) That insight from one who endured so much ought to tell us something about the cadence that will, at times, be called in our individual lives.

The Prophet Joseph Smith and a large body of men moved overland in Zion's Camp. It was in an episode that the Lord described at one point as their having been brought "thus far for a trial of their faith." (D&C 105:19.) Should we not more often reflect upon what is really going on in life—the growth and improvement of individuals—other explanations notwithstanding?

Is it not wise, from time to time, to reflect upon the case studies in the scriptures? For instance, we can see Joseph Smith in the midst of his ordeal in Liberty Jail being reminded that "all these things shall give thee experience, and shall be for thy good." (D&C 122:7.) We have not only our own experiences to draw upon, but also the experiences of those in the scriptures. We can learn vicariously by drawing upon the wisdom of the scriptures; each age does not have to have its Sodom and Gomorrah.

True, if we fail to profit from the experience of others and to learn from the lessons that "the tides of history wash to our feet," then we are very likely to repeat those mistakes (or some variation thereof) with the same awful pain.

One of the marvelous features, however, of the atonement of Jesus Christ is that he who suffered so greatly that he bled from every pore can, under certain prescribed conditions, spare us the need to suffer personally even as he suffered. This is, of course, the marvelous grace of Christ that is so generously proffered to us. Using that grace depends so much on our doing what John Taylor suggested when he urged us to "act for eternity"—to behave in a manner that acknowledges eternity as a reality.

The aforementioned Doctors Friedman and Rosenman have counseled men about how they might alter a life-style that, unchanged, often foreshadows a heart attack. There may well be "Type A" families, too, that also have certain behavioral patterns that emphasize "vocal expressiveness," rapidity of action, impatience, doing too many things simultaneously, selfishness, inability to relax and to make wise use of leisure time, inability to appreciate the lovely things in one's environment (taking time to smell flowers), too much acquisitiveness with regard to material things, a sense of time urgency, too much competitiveness, and too much preoccupation with speed when slowness, in some situations, is the way in which much of the beauty of life is revealed.

Of course, too much can be made of the physiological and psychological parallels, but in the one case, "Type A" physical and emotional behavior can bring a heart attack to an individual. In the other, unhealthy behavior in a family brings heartbreaks.

Perhaps the childlike qualities that are so compatible with heaven in so many other ways also include the rejection of franticness as described in this child's view of life:

> *I don't like a world of muchness,*
> *A world of push and fast and no;*
> *I like a world of swept-out bigness,*
> *Of let and think and slow.*

Perpetually frantic families are deficient in "let and think and slow"; they also lack parental poise.

In Proverbs we read, "He that hath no rule over his own spirit is like a city that is broken down, and without walls." (Proverbs 25:28.) The imagery invoked is that of vulnerability. Frantic families (those that, without rule over their own spirits, lack adequate direction and adequate discipline, are too accessible to outsiders, and are too trampled upon by urgencies) are also like a "city that is broken down and without walls."

CHAPTER SIX

Be Ye Not Unequally Yoked Together

S uccessful parenthood depends, more than we care to admit, on our being able to succeed as a wife or as a husband. Our children, seeing the sermon of our actual behavior (more than hearing what we say), are bound to make their own assessment of our relationship as parents. John Donne wrote: "The subsequent life is the best printing and the most useful and profitable publishing of a Sermon."

What follows is obviously not a comprehensive effort to deal with this vital matter, but, rather, a few suggestions.

First, it is perhaps useful for us as partners to identify a few samples of the little things that we sometimes let get in the way of a richer and deeper marriage. Of course, little things, in a sense, are the big things, but we sometimes brush them aside as mere symptoms of something that doesn't really need to be treated, because we think of these things as being little; hence, the possible value of the mundane assessment that follows.

Select *two* of the tendencies, from among those that follow, that could enrich your relationship with your mate were you to eliminate them. Reflect *privately* and candidly on your performance and behavior, not with the idea that it is grossly wrong or sinisterly deficient, but rather, with the idea that it can be improved considerably by the cumulative consequences of small, specific improvements.

_____**A.** I tend at times to use humor as a vehicle for giving verbal stings to my partner.

_____**B.** I tend at times to impose the silent treatment on my partner.

_____**C.** I have a tendency at times to withhold affection and verbal support from my mate because I feel aggrieved.

_____**D.** I have a tendency to withhold help from my mate when the tasks that are considered to be mine in our marriage are done, even though my partner's remain undone and help is obviously needed.

_____**E.** I have a tendency not to express, specifically and regularly, my love and respect for my mate, thinking perhaps that frequent expression is not necessary, or perhaps because by withholding I serve notice in order to get some of my concerns out on the table.

_____**F.** Occasionally I undercut my mate in front of the children, rather than dealing with such matters, if these arise, more appropriately in the privacy of our marriage.

_____**G.** I have a tendency to under-disclose in terms of my expectations and hopes so that my partner often isn't fully aware of either my frustrations or my aspirations.

_____**H.** I have a tendency at times to unload my problems and personal crises (from either the office or the home) on my partner without reflecting on whether or not he, or she, can at that time manage the added load and/or without reflecting on the possibility that I need to provide a parallel opportunity for my partner to share the cumulative load that he, or she, has acquired.

_____**I.** I have a tendency, in one respect or another, to build a private little world into which I sometimes retreat, leaving my partner standing outside.

_____**J.** I have a tendency to be overly concerned with material and financial matters and to press these concerns a little too much in our marriage.

_____**K.** I have a tendency to be under-concerned about financial matters in our marriage, leaving that responsibility too much to my partner.
_____**L.** Other (please specify)._____

Having chosen two such things in which one could do better, the next step in this exercise is equally simple. It consists of narrowing the choice to just *one* selection and then asking oneself simply, "In order to improve in this regard, what one thing could I *stop* doing?" (List) _____.
"What one thing could I *start* doing?" (List) _____
_____. The block that the above patterns may constitute to a richer and deeper marriage may be simple, but by pondering and then committing to improve, a minor block could be made into a stepping stone.

Since marriage is not static—it is an evolving thing—sometimes it is useful for us as couples, when we see the challenges that still lie ahead, to look back at our climb to see how far we have come. Just one way of involving husband and wife in mutual communication on this issue would be for each of the spouses to first identify *two* things they as a couple have accomplished in their marriage in the last five (or two) years that are most significant. (This reflecting, at first individually, if done seriously and sincerely, should then be shared with each other for discussion.) There may not be, of course, a perfect match of the things that are selected as indicators of past success, but such a brief exercise in reflecting and sharing can be encouraging to both partners in a marriage. They can see themselves get credited with some successes. It is also helpful to know what the other person in the partnership cherishes by way of past successes, which of course can give some helpful clues to the future.

There may be some unevenness in the significance in the things so selected, but that in itself can be something that husband and wife can discuss. Such an inventory also permits a couple to make allowance for the various periods of challenge through which the family and a marriage pass. President David O. McKay, for instance, described the early years of marriage as the years of economic struggle, referring to what is usually a more Spartan period in terms of the material and financial resources of a newly married couple.

Success is contagious. Sometimes we need to be reminded of what we have achieved. This can give us fresh courage and determination to succeed again, whatever our current challenges may be. A little reflection, therefore, is worthwhile, especially when it can be undertaken in a spirit of happiness, cooperation, and communication.

Although goal setting can clearly be overdone, only a few people are overly involved with goals and goal setting; most people do far too little goal setting, including the reflecting that precedes the setting of such goals. Too many marriages have financial goals but not other explicit goals. Yet the gospel is certainly goal-oriented.

The late Elder Richard L. Evans was fond of saying that if one was not certain as to where he was going, it didn't matter if he got there.

A vague goal is no goal at all. The Ten Commandments wouldn't be very impressive, for instance, if they weren't specific, but simply were couched in a phraseology such as "thou shalt not be a bad person." Just as those who believe in a vague, remote, unknowable God who is undemanding of them don't really have a religion at all; just as those who feature vagueness in their communications instead of accuracy don't really care about others involved in the process of communication, so vagueness in goal setting and vagueness in perceiving what has occurred or been achieved can produce a marital relationship in which there is coexistence rather than cooperation; in which there is survival but not satisfaction; in which there is proximity but not intimacy.

There are some positive little things we can do that, of course, are really big things in the last analysis. A husband or a wife already knows (but if not, can quickly determine) what things, what small gestures, may give special satisfaction to his or her partner. For a wife this may be receiving occasional flowers as a surprise from the husband. For a husband, it may be the wife's fixing of a special dish.

In a sense what is done, specifically, doesn't matter so much as that something specific is done, something that attests to our continued desire to please our partner. Such little acts let the recipient know that we *do* think of them and have given some thought to, and have taken some satisfaction in, doing something that pleases them.

A wife may request a walk around the block but find her husband too busy to want to go. When such a clue has been given several times, it would be well if the husband would find time to take that walk anyway and, moreover, suggest it himself, spontaneously.

A husband who is concerned with budget matters and struggling with making his money span across the family needs may, on occasion, neglect his own need for a new pair of shoes, for instance. He may resist the expenditure nobly. To have the wife take that burden of decision from him, letting him know how much the family appreciates his self-denial in their behalf but that they think that his turn has come, can help build up his feelings of love and acceptance.

Instead of the sometimes petty humor one sees in social situations, such as when the husband puts down the wife, one might also make a special effort to give a deserved, specific compliment to his partner in a setting that matters to both of them, not in a manipulative or superficial way or simply for effect, but genuinely and deservingly. Spontaneously given compliments, however, are normally not spontaneous as to their content; they come out of reflection and accumulated appreciation. Compliments can be harvested for spontaneous use but the crop needs specific preparation and cultivation in order to be ready for the plucking.

Of course, there has to be, first, a desire to do the little things in marriage. If that desire is absent, no number of suggestions as to technique will work. With that desire, however, much better suggestions than these above can surely be found.

A relationship between husband and wife that is characterized by a generosity of spirit and by selflessness can overcome anything that is placed in its path. Meanwhile, a happy marriage gets noticed, not only by the children, but by ever so many others who can (and who desperately need to) see a successful marriage.

There are men and women who don't succeed in marriage but who at least succeed at other things. We sometimes make the mistake, however, of thinking that notable successes outside their marriage and family are more important. Anyone, however, who understands the gospel would have to see those successes as a kind of consolation prize in which a generous God is anxious to reward those involved for the use they make of the talents they have as fully as he possibly can. But when the secular applause has died down and the bands have stopped playing—when the mortal measuring of those compensatory successes has concluded—such individuals are often left with a tragic emptiness (insofar as eternal things are concerned), "for they have their reward."

Perspective about our parental partnerships can keep us free from folly of all sorts, such as the fashionable denigration of our parental roles. Note the wisdom of C. S. Lewis:

> *I think I can understand that feeling about a housewife's work being like that of Sisyphus, (who was the stone-rolling gentleman). But it is surely in reality the most important work in the world. What do ships, railways, mines, cars, government, etc. exist for except that people may be fed, warmed, and safe in their own homes? As Dr. Johnson said, "To be happy at home is the end of all human endeavor." (1st, to be happy to prepare for being happy in our own real home hereafter; 2nd, in the meantime to be happy in our houses.) We wage war in order to have peace, we work in order to have leisure, we produce food in order to eat it. So your job is the one for which all others exist. . . .* (Letters of C. S. Lewis, *London: Godfrey Bles Ltd., p. 262.*)

Being equally yoked together in family life involves more than just the cooperation of husband and wife—it also involves the children in the family. Leaders have responsibilities, but so do followers; children also have duties and obligations. We appear, at least in the United States, to be coming out of a period in which many parents were too child-centered, and that period generated unusual parental anxiety to please and also some undeserved self-condemnation by parents. Parents who crave the approval of their children at the expense of principle will find that they worship a jealous and capricious god. Parents who do too much *for* their children will usually find that they cannot do anything *with* their children, neither in establishing suitable standards nor in sharing experiences.

In the interest of stressing sons' and daughters' responsibilities, the exercise below provides a sample way that children (at least those old enough to respond) may inventory some of their own attitudes about family life.

Youthful or young-adult members of a family in an appropriate setting select those two of the following tendencies that most accurately describe their most frequent failure in family life:

_____**A.** I have a tendency to regard the home as a personal hotel designed to meet my needs for food, shelter, clean clothes, and a chance to regroup before leaving again—and am sometimes impatient with the help.

_____**B.** I have a tendency to direct conversations and family attention toward my needs and concerns with too little concern for the needs of other family members.

_____**C.** I have a tendency to let my boredom show and/or to be condescending to my parents and/or my younger brothers/sisters, in attitude, voice tone, and comments.

_____**D.** I have a tendency to be too much at the mercy of my moods and pass these along and through the family.

_____**E.** I seldom give deserved, specific commendation to other members of the family.

_____**F.** I have a tendency to worry too little about the financial challenges of my parents and what I might do to alleviate these.

_____**G.** I seldom express genuine satisfaction in the achievements of other family members or genuine concern over their trials and disappointments.

_____**H.** I have a tendency to mutter and groan over some of the tasks and chores I am given to do.

_____**I.** I have a tendency to be vague about my plans in my communications with my parents.

_____**J.** I am not as good a listener as I expect my parents to be.

_____**K.** I have a tendency not to be a self-starter; nevertheless, I sometimes resent my parents' reminders about things I need to get done.

_____**L.** I have a tendency to withhold affection and love from my parents even when I know they hunger for such.

_____**M.** I have a tendency to let myself appear less committed to the Church and to gospel values than I really am, doing this sometimes to irritate my parents.

_____**N.** I have a tendency to tune out parental advice (even when I sense or know it is valid) because I dislike how or when my parents give this advice to me.

_____**O.** I seldom deliberately ask my parents to give me counsel or advice.

_____**P.** I am simply too uninvolved in my family to contribute or even to have real commitment thereto.

_____**Q.** I expect my parents to make allowance for my moods or crises, but seldom do I do the same for them.

_____**R.** Other (please specify) _____
_____

If I, as a youth or young adult, wish to do more to enrich my family life, I will now work on just *one* of the two needs for improvement that I selected (list which one) and commit myself to strive for significant improvement. In order to do this I will *start* _____
(list one specific thing you will start doing)
and I will also *stop* _____as evidence
(list one specific thing you will start doing)
of my fresh effort to improve.

Though perhaps some of it is to be expected, few things are as hard for parents to bear as chronic indifference, ingratitude, and insensitivity on the part of their sons and daughters. Next in order of tragicness to the child who has seldom or never heard from parents the words "I love you" are those parents who have seldom or never heard those words from their children. In contrast, consider how in the moments of exquisite agony—indescribable agony—a model Son on the cross at Calvary lovingly managed to make arrangements for the welfare of his mother, Mary.

There are circumstances wherein young men and women consciously put their parents through the calisthenics of concern. Often in these circumstances the young don't disbelieve at all, but for varied reasons they are not willing to have their parents be too comfortable about the status of their souls. Perhaps the young are simply probing and testing to see if their parents really believe and how deep their faith is. Another possibility is that the young are anxious for their parents to be better than the parents are, hence the youthful pressing of the parents into better behavior by holding themselves back until the parents pay the ransom and become what they pretend to be. Whatever the motivation, this is a form of youthful hypocrisy: the better known form of hypocrisy, Fosdick has told us, is pretending to be better than we are, but the other form is letting ourselves appear to be worse or less committed than we are.

Parents would sometimes do well to confront kindly their sons and daughters if such behavior does arise. Other times, a good case can be made for simply letting young people work this out, as long as there is no parental failure to call attention to standards or sin when necessary. Some such things may well fall within the zone of indifference, since if parents overreact, they may simply start a chain reaction that puts more distance between themselves and their children.

Often the best communication link in such a situation may be a teenager's just slightly older brother or sister who has worked his or her way through this period of time and who can make sibling sense to the younger. Nevertheless, just as politicians, while running for election, aren't sure the bumper stickers help; aren't sure whether the billboard advertising is really effective; aren't sure that radio and TV spots are worth the cost; aren't sure that running about small hamlets and villages to speak is a good idea—they are afraid not to do these things for fear that these might make a difference—so parents are sometimes left with little choice except to be anxious lest in their seeming indifference they overlook doing something that might help in such an impasse.

CHAPTER SEVEN

The Spirit of Revelation

*T*he need for operational inspiration and revelation in our lives and in our families cannot be overemphasized. Regular communications from one individual to another must pass through our finite filtering screens of past experience, our stereotypes, and our prejudices. Little wonder, for instance, that an idea so grand and so new as the resurrection was hard for even those who were close to Jesus to understand. Such powerful ideas require us, in a sense, to leap outside the confines of time, space, and experience. One of the vital roles of revelation is to help us to do just this—something neither reason nor experience can do for us, for these other two vital methods of knowing have this serious limitation.

The Spirit can impel an idea or insight into our soul as if by shortcut without the usual processing by which we encode and decode communications. The Spirit can give us a sudden, blinding, flashing insight about ourselves. For instance, we may suddenly see a shortcoming—a perception that might otherwise never make it through our defensiveness or our mesh of misunderstanding. The Spirit can also permit us to understand a truth, or at least know something *is* true, even if we don't understand the full implications of that truth. When we know that a truth is from a divine source, there can be a resonance deep inside ourselves that causes us to listen reverentially, even if we do not understand fully the consequences of that communication. Obviously, in such situations, the efficiency of communication reaches its near zenith, for we are not encumbered with our finite experiential limitations, nor are we hemmed in by the revetments of reason. We find ourselves suddenly lifted above the terrace of time and onto the edge of eternity. In no dimension of our lives is operational inspiration more regularly needed than in the management of our families; nor is the significance of this need merely in its regularity; it is also in its cruciality.

So often in the mundane matters of life what we really need is perspective about ourselves and our situations. Shakespeare, in *Henry V,* has the military leader plead with his gallant little band, who await a day of battle, to see themselves not pessimistically, but as being in an especially influential position; to think of themselves as having not a special problem, but a special opportunity. Later, those participants who fought and "come home safe" would "stand a tip-toe when this day is nam'd,"

> *And gentlemen in England, now a-bed*
> *Shall think themselves accurs'd they were not here,*
> *And hold their manhoods cheap whiles any speaks*
> *That fought with us upon St. Crispin's day.*
> *—Act 4, scene 3*

So often we are intimidated by our ignorance. In seeing segments we see things too separately, not in their proper relationship to each other. The prophet Elisha's young servant, lacking perspective and feeling encompassed by the enemy host, uttered aloud, "Alas, my master! how shall we do?" (2 Kings 6:15.) Or in another instance, the scout sent out by ancient Israel saw the giant sons of Anak and reported fearfully and candidly, ". . . we were in our own sight as grasshoppers, and so we were in their sight." (Numbers 13:33.)

Sometimes opposition is undeservedly intimidating simply because we do not know of or use the resources available to us with which to deal with that challenge; we lack the perspective necessary to place that challenge in proper perspective. It was G. K. Chesterton who asserted that the humble man often sees big things because, first of all, he strains his eyes more than the average man in order to see what other men miss. Second, the humble man is both genuinely overwhelmed and uplifted by his adventures in wider perspective. Third, the humble man is apt to record such remarkable experiences (in his mind and for others) more accurately than if he were processing these experiences through proud, perceptual screens.

One cannot read of Moses, though raised in a royal court, still being described in the scriptures as "very meek, above all the men which were upon the face of the earth" (Numbers 12:3), without pondering the importance of meekness, since the meek shall inherit the earth.

We should ponder Thoreau's statement that "humility, like darkness, reveals the heavenly lights." In elaborating on this, Leonard B. Reed concluded that meekness relates more than anything else to teachability and therefore, "the teachable shall be graced with the realization of their earthly potentials."

Teachableness puts man in a relationship to truth in which he does not flinch from the implications of the truth, but is open to receive it. Thus being realistic, the humble man can cope with this world and with the world to come with greater competency than those who are not teachable.

The Spirit's adventures come to the teachable and to the shy. Pride not only dries up laughter, but our capacity to ponder and to wonder as well.

There may be some correlation in all of this with the frequency in history with which the young have done so much, so ably, so well, so soon. It was Benjamin Disraeli who once said, "Almost everything that is great has been done by youth."

This appears to have been true whether one is talking about Michelangelo, Beethoven, Rembrandt, or Alexander the Great. While the lack of previous experience handicaps youth, previous experience can also hold hostage those who are older, preventing us from having or appreciating fresh experiences that could help us to restructure more correctly our understanding of the nature of the world and of life.

God gave to mankind through a young man, Joseph Smith, the ultimate and immense truths of the gospel in this, the last dispensation. This young man who had no social status to protect, no private theology already worked out for God to endorse, and who had loving and listening parents, could report that theophany honestly and cling tenaciously to the truth of that first vision in the midst of great persecution. A sophisticated man who had community status to protect and his own ideas about what kind of religion the world needed— even though a good man—would have been sorely tempted to have traded off truth for the praise of the world. Paul reminded us that "the friendship of the world is enmity with God. . . ." (James 4:4.) Could any but a humble non-linguist have gone to the Hill Cumorah and, under the direction of an angel, be shown ancient records and be told, so boldly, that he, personally, would be the unlettered instrument in translating these for the benefit of all mankind, and still have believed all that—and helped such a marvel come to pass without wanting somehow to possess the plates rather than share their wisdom or to add his own mortal touches and flourishes to the manuscript?

In relation to his calling, Joseph Smith no doubt stood much like Enoch and Moses: overwhelmed that he had been chosen, but, nevertheless, humbly determined to do just what was asked of him. To the humble, the simpleness and the easiness of the way are glad realities; to the crowded, ego-filled minds of proud men, the sudden sunlight from a spiritual sunrise is irritating rather than awesome, and causes them to blink rather than to stare in reverent awe.

President Marion G. Romney has indicated how truly important it is that we have inspiration even in initiating our prayerful petitions. The Book of Mormon tells us that our prayers are subject not only to our faith, but also to the criteria by which God determines if we ask for something that is right. Elsewhere we are told to ask only for those things which are expedient for us, and that the Holy Ghost manifests all things that are expedient. And in section 46, verse 30, of the Doctrine and Covenants, with regard to our praying, we are advised of a powerful reality, that one who "asketh in the Spirit asketh according to the will of God; wherefore it is done even as he asketh."

It isn't simply a case of having the pass key of faith to unlock the treasures of heaven from which we can then extract whatever blessing we choose; we need the Spirit operating in our lives to shape our very desires and hence our very requests, *but* on the basis of what is really good for us.

Where better than in the family can we learn of prayer and the realities facing our petitions? A number of years ago, President Spencer W. Kimball observed soberingly that "the answer to some of our prayers would destroy us," calling attention to our need to remember that our prayers are petitions after all.

The Spirit is even able to facilitate what President Joseph F. Smith called the "education of our desires."

The access to the Spirit does another important thing for us as well: it can give us the humility about ourselves and our circumstances that makes it less likely that we will overreact when we are offended, less likely that we will strike out at others on trivial matters. The presence of the Spirit in our lives also permits us to remember, and to be grateful for, past benefactors and past favors. The world's way, of course, is one in which new grievances quickly drain our reservoirs of gratitude.

Further, the presence of the Holy Ghost in one's life, insofar as it reshapes our desires and our appetites, can move us from a position in which, at first, we wisely avoid temptations, to a point finally from which the things alien to the Spirit of God are diminished in their attractiveness. Just as what is at first a duty can later become a delight, so the dangerous things for which we may now hunger can be replaced by desires for things that are not only harmless, but that will also help us.

Access to the Spirit can also give us the extra wisdom in tactical situations where we might otherwise be swept along with the herd. Just because some among us today are pleading and cajoling for more and more freedom to drive themselves mad, those who do not wish to join any such march of the lemmings should not have to. But that happy decision to resist being steered along with the herd will need constant reinforcement, and the Spirit can give such to each of us.

Perhaps, too, one of the most important functions of the Spirit in our lives is to remind and warn us about what we already know and of our need to avoid the things that are sinful.

It was John Donne who concluded, "Here then the Holy Ghost takes the nicest way to bring a man to God, by awaking his memory."

Elsewhere Donne makes the same kind of observation about the interaction of the Holy Ghost with our memory when he observes that "that Memory is oftener the Holy Ghost's Pulpit that he preaches in, than the Understanding," and memory is described as "the stomach of the soul," which receives, digests, and assimilates the blessings we receive from God.

The Holy Ghost can also fill us with justified hope when things seem hopeless. The Reverend Ernest T. Campbell wrote interestingly about Peter who, at one point—certainly not the point of his spiritual apogee—was described in the scriptures as follows: "But Peter followed him at a distance, as far as the courtyard of the high priest, and going inside he sat with the guards to see the end."

One can only guess at the thoughts that filled Peter's bosom on that lonely night. There can be an immobility when despair clasps us tightly to its bosom. Of this parallel, the Reverend Campbell wrote: "Millions in our world today sit where Peter sat that night—to see the end. Disillusionment blankets many and many a heart. The feeling persists that some grim inevitability is moving in upon us. That it's just a matter of time. And so we sit to watch the end." (*Christian World,* April 1974, p. 4.)

The perspectives of the gospel can give us a fresh vision, not alone of what we are, but of what we have the power to become; not just a clear picture of our circumstance, but a clear view of what our circumstances could become.

Insofar as the Spirit promotes in us a love of our fellow-man, it can increase our capacity for empathy. Nor does one save the inspiration of the Spirit only for the so-called "big things," for as Wilferd A. Peterson has observed, "In the art of marriage the little things are the big things. . . ." (*The New Book of the Art of Living.*) Having the help of the Holy Ghost in coping with little things (as in one's need to be more patient) can be a great help.

The Spirit can purify our love, can lift it from the levels of eroticism or mere friendship and affection to the level of charity, which love has been described as "the perfect antidote that floods the mind to wash away hatred, jealousy, resentment, anxiety and fear."

The Spirit can also prepare us for adventures from which we would surely shrink without the assurances and preparation that precede them.

It was C. S. Lewis who observed of what implications lay behind the eloquent expression of the suffering Savior ("Why hast thou forsaken me?"):

> *There is a mystery here which, even if I had the power, I might not have the courage to explore. Meanwhile, little people like you and me, if our prayers are sometimes granted beyond all hope and probability, had better not draw hasty conclusions to our own advantage. If we were stronger, we might be less tenderly treated. If we were braver, we might be sent, with far less help, to defend far more desperate posts in the great battle.* (The World's Last Night, *New York: Harcourt Brace, 1960, pp. 10-11.*)

Just as an unsheltered flame flutters when it is brushed by gusts of wind, and just as the unsheltered flame sputters when dashed by rain, we as individuals need to avoid deliberately those "desperate posts" for which we are not ready, those conditions which deprive us of access to the Spirit and which dampen our light. But, in addition to avoidance, we also need to create and search out those conditions in which our light can burn more brightly and steadily. We need an appropriate blend of challenge and refuge, of search and sanctuary; we need to create and to preserve the proper conditions for burning. The flame of family can warm us and at the same time be a perpetual pilot light to rekindle us.

This matter, therefore, of being a light is even more important in dark times. Our impact, for better or worse, on others is inevitable, but it is intended that we be a light and not just another shadow.

The same God that placed that star in a precise orbit millennia before it appeared over Bethlehem in celebration of the birth of the Babe has given at least equal attention to placement of each of us in precise human orbits so that we may, if we will, illuminate the landscape of our individual lives, so that our light may not only lead others but warm them as well.

For all of this, we must have the gift of the Holy Ghost. But the Holy Ghost never waits to leave until he is formally asked to leave, for his influence has already departed even as we, by our thoughts, slide toward sin.

The Spirit can both help us to decide and remind us relentlessly of past decisions to choose the good. Perhaps one of the impasses that individuals encounter when they wish to do good is their failure to decide also on what they will *not* do; such temporizing on one flank (indecision about what we will not do) imperils the other flank (what we ought to do) by robbing us of full vigor. Note how, once again, we must put truth at the center, if we are to act with certitude.

It was Count Leo Tolstoy who said of the efforts to have morality independent of true religion (and such efforts are much more common today) that such attempts "are like the actions of children when, wishing to move a plant which pleases them, they tear off the root which does not please, and seems unnecessary to them, and plant it in the earth without the root. Without a religious foundation there can be no true, sincere morality, as without a root there can be no true plant."

Michael Polanyi has perceptively observed that much of modern fanaticism "is rooted in an extreme skepticism which can only be strengthened, not shaken, by further doses of universal doubt." He has also observed that "the freedom of the subjective person to do as he pleases is overruled by the freedom of the responsible person to act as he must." (*Personal Knowledge,* New York: Harper Torchbooks, 1964.) But to act as we must requires direction and courage, both of which can come from the Holy Ghost.

There is probably a significant link between the idea of a straight and narrow path and the need for maintaining balance in our lives, which balance can best be maintained by the influence of the Holy Ghost to guide us and to keep us from veering too much to the right or the left. Most commonly, the course corrections we need in our lives are not dramatic, but are small, *if* we make them *as* we should and *when* we should. But the unadjusted error, however minor, when persisted in will take us a great way off the straight and narrow path.

Having passion for what we know is true brings us into a relationship with God that beckons us to come even closer to him. The Spirit can let us inside, so to speak, as we deal with holy things. George Macdonald once said, "Nothing is so deadening to the divine as a habitual dealing with the outsides of holy things." He also concluded with regard to his desire for closeness to God, "I would go near Thee—but I cannot press into Thy presence. . . . Thy doors are deeds."

Elder Bruce R. McConkie has stated that "service is essential to salvation." Deeds *do* matter as well as doctrines, but the doctrines can move us to do the deeds, and the Spirit can help us to understand the doctrines as well as prompt us to do the deeds.

Indeed, the magnification of our individual callings, inside and outside the family, depends upon our access to the power of God. Brigham Young said an individual "must speak by the power of God or he does not magnify his calling."

We need the Spirit to bring us to understanding. In *Gracian's Manual* we read: "To jog the understanding is a greater feat than to jog the memory: for it takes more to make a man think, than to make him remember." (Martin Fischer, publisher, p. 92.)

The Spirit, by moving us to action, can bless us, too, with wisdom as to timing. We also read in *Gracian's Manual,* "A wise man does at once what a fool does last. Both do the same thing; only at different times, the first in season, the second out." (Ibid., p. 93.) Surely, in the rigors of family life, we need to be inspired not only as to what we do, and how we do it, but also as to when.

If we continue to have access to the Spirit to guide us in our performance, then when we perform anything, we will do it in such a manner that God "will consecrate thy performance unto thee, that thy performance may be for the welfare of thy soul." (2 Nephi 32:9.) What an incredible insight this is!

Since God has declared that his whole labor is to "bring to pass the immortality and eternal life of man," it is an even further sublime act of love that God will help us in such a way that our performance—our acts and thoughts—may be "for the welfare of thy soul." In a secular world full of unintended counter-productiveness, of pyrrhic victories, and of solutions that turn into problems, how reassuring!

An example of the cosmic chemistry that is involved when this divine guidance lights the way, one of those special moments, occurred in the episode involving King Lamoni and the missionary efforts of Ammon. Ammon, looking on, knew "that king Lamoni was under the power of God; he knew that the dark veil of unbelief was being cast away from his mind, and the light which did light up his mind, which was the light of the glory of God, which was a marvelous light of his goodness —yea, this light had infused such joy into his soul, the cloud of darkness having been dispelled, and that the light of everlasting life was lit up in his soul, yea, he knew that this had overcome his natural frame, and he was carried away in God." (Alma 19:6.)

Elder Delbert L. Stapley of the Council of the Twelve has observed, fittingly, "When the light of Christ is in one's soul there can be no darkness which leads to temptation and sin. You cannot take darkness into a lighted room any more than one can create doubt in the heart of a person where true faith and testimony exist."

God has reminded us that it is possible for men to love darkness rather than light. One has to assume that those who do evil hate the light not only because it exposes them, but because they have grown grumblingly used to the darkness.

In the short run, the children of darkness make no bones about what kind of choices they have made. Their actions are not tentative. They work feverishly "in their generation." From an eternal perspective the children of light have, of course, made the right choice. However, having made that choice, their task now is to pursue it with the same kind of tenacity, energy, and dedication with which the children of darkness pursue their value system.

Too much tentativeness leads to "giveupitis," a human phenomenon to which Jesus called attention with regard to those fair-weather followers of John the Baptist. Jesus described John as "a burning and a shining light: and ye were willing for a season to rejoice in his light." (John 5:35.) Staying power, rather than seasonal rejoicing, is another great task for the disciple of Jesus for which we need the gift of the Holy Ghost.

John Donne made the point that, first, the grace of God means that he never forsakes us; and next, God's "helping graces" come to us to help, not to forsake ourselves! Or our families!

CHAPTER EIGHT

A House of Friends

*M*any of today's college students seem to be seeking enduring commitments but prefer human relationships to ideologies. Can one expect human relationships to be deep and lasting sources of purpose and meaning without having truth at their center? Can there be friendships such as the friendship of Jonathan and David outside the context of absolute values? We read that "Jonathan was knit with the soul of David"; these two individuals "made a covenant." (See 1 Samuel 18:1-3.)

Friendships formed in the context of floating values are apt to be floating friendships—devoid of real acceptance, depth, and continuity, the very things that friendship is intended to supply in the first place.

When humans are thrown together in more and more temporary relationships in which selfishness is emphasized, in which sensation is sought, we will constantly disappoint each other because we will always be taking. Can we build real friendships without knowing who we are? Strangers may interact at the level of sensation, but not usually at the levels of knowing and loving.

Families in which the individual members are also friends are not only a joy *per se,* but these families prepare friends for us all. Perhaps there have been too many homes in the past that were too authoritarian, in which parents were not adequately respectful of their children, for homes must rest upon a foundation of mutual respect, just as democratic institutions require a shared concern to succeed. In any event, shared and correct understanding about what life is all about greatly facilitates friendship in and out of families.

The increasing and cruel phenomenon of parents who do not like children needs no elaboration here. Some chronically prevent childbirth; others brutalize children after they come; still others ignore children. All such feature not friendship within families, but forms of fratricide.

The great preventive forces contained in the gospel of Jesus Christ and in its premises about the nature of man and of life permit parents and children to avoid metronomic swings between coddling children too much and the tendency to push children out of the nest too soon and too harshly.

An article in *Newsweek* (March 4, 1974) observed:

In the most recent cycle, grown-ups moved from the cold remote authoritarianism of the Victorian Era, with its insistence on obedience, moral abstinence and emotional sublimation, to the closely attentive permissiveness of the twentieth century, with its emphasis on spontaneity, moral relativism, and emotional expression. To put it more bluntly, while Victorian parents responded entirely to their own feelings, modern parents have responded only to their children's feelings—and neither system worked very well.

The stories of various sibling relationships that are such a primary part of family life have been too well treated to require repetition here, but one cannot help but be struck by the nobility of a man like Hyrum Smith, an older brother, who made room for a younger brother, Joseph Smith. Hyrum gladly supported his younger brother in the marvelous things Joseph had to do, glorying in the younger brother's achievements and sharing, finally, even martyrdom as a brother. These men were "knit together," as were David and Jonathan.

Why in such cases could there be such sibling love and loyalty, when there was so much hatred by Cain for Abel? Or, in the case of the older brothers Laman and Lemuel, why the bitter hatred and envy they felt at certain points of their life for their younger brother, Nephi, for whom they made absolutely no allowance? Did Laman's jealousy of Nephi block the development of Laman's faith, or did his lack of faith make him jealous of Nephi? Is there some common factor that explains, too, the case of the older brothers of Joseph of the Old Testament?

A whole study could be made about brothers in scriptural history. Even in our time, we saw in the late and sweet Elder Thomas E. McKay a "Hyrum" who made room for and supported a special brother, President David O. McKay.

No doubt many things account for the sweetness of some brothers and the hatred of others. Part of the explanation has to lie in the capacity of these individuals to accept the realities of the gospel truths that are provided as an accurate explanation and interpretation of life. Cain, for instance, could not cope with rejection. Though we do not have many details of the episode involving his murder of his younger brother, we know enough to know that Cain was caught making an offering that did not comply with the standards that had been openly set. Whatever pattern of jealousy and differential faith there had been between these two siblings in the years preceding this awful tragedy, it is clear enough (see the fourth chapter of Genesis) that even remonstration with Cain about the conditions under which his sacrifice could still be accepted was not adequate to turn his darkening thoughts into brighter paths.

We see generosity of spirit in the life of Abraham when he and Lot, who was his nephew, found their cattle grazing on the same land. There was strife between the herdsmen of Abraham's cattle and of Lot's cattle. It is Abraham who took the initiative and said unto Lot, "Let there be no strife, I pray thee, between me and thee, and between my herdmen and thy herdmen; for we be brethren. Is not the whole land before thee? separate thyself, I pray thee, from me: if thou wilt take the left hand, then I will go to the right; or if thou depart to the right hand, then I will go to the left." (Genesis 13:7-9.) The complete, genuine willingness of Abraham to adjust to whatever Lot's decision was is the mark of a generosity of spirit of that remarkable patriarch.

Even in a small way our own capacity to deal with family feedback becomes a fresh departure point for the outstanding person and a deep pit for those who cannot handle it. It is easy, of course, given our own experiences, to imagine how hard it must have been for two older brothers, Laman and Lemuel, to have Nephi preach to them. Yet at the same time, there is an important clue in their reaction on one occasion (1 Nephi 16) when Nephi concluded his remonstrations: Laman and Lemuel said, "Thou hast declared unto us hard things, more than we are able to bear. . . ." Nephi observed on that occasion, "the guilty taketh the truth to be hard, for it cutteth them to the very center." Laman and Lemuel apparently had difficulty dealing with both the cosmic and the personal implications of the truths Nephi spoke to them.

There were, of course, moments of episodic humility even with Laman and Lemuel, but they were never quite able to commit themselves to a full acceptance of the truth, either theologically or behaviorally. It is easy, too, to see how the younger brother Joseph, in a sense, was put to a similar disadvantage with his brothers because their father's preference showed that "Israel loved Joseph more than all his children, because he was the son of his old age: and he made him a coat of many colours." (Genesis 37:3.) Seeing this, Joseph's brothers "saw that their father loved him more than all his brethren, they hated him, and could not speak peaceably unto him." (Genesis 37:4.) Moreover, they resented Joseph's dream, which, of course, foreshadowed his dominion over them. "And they hated him yet the more for his dreams, and for his words." (Genesis 37:8.) To what extent, if any, the young Joseph exploited his special status, we do not know.

Touching and revealing is the later episode (Genesis 42)

when Joseph recognizes his brothers (though they did not recognize him) and again, in a generosity of spirit, helps them to buy much-needed corn. Touching, too, is the weeping of Joseph in the course of his later dialogue with the brothers. The multiple weepings of Joseph preparatory to his eventual recognition by his brothers tell us a great deal about this remarkable man, who is one of the most impressive characters in all of recorded history. Joseph "could not refrain himself" from disclosing who he really was after displaying great generosity of spirit toward them who had grieved him. At this point, the scriptures record these moving words: "And he fell upon his brother Benjamin's neck, and wept; and Benjamin wept upon his neck. Moreover he kissed *all his brethren,* and wept upon them: and after that his brethren talked with him." (Genesis 45:14-15. Italics added.)

Few families have seen more drama than the family of Jacob, and seldom has there been more gallant and timely exit than Jacob's: "And when Jacob had made an end of commanding his sons, he gathered up his feet into the bed, and yielded up the ghost, and was gathered unto his people." (Genesis 49:33.)

Then Joseph "fell upon his father's face, and wept upon him, and kissed him." (Genesis 50:1.)

Note in this episode Joseph's generosity of spirit, his commitment to absolute truth, his selflessness, his sense of history, and his patience, all of which are virtues that ought to be in every family.

It is significant, too, that even after such a rapprochement Joseph's brethren wondered after their father died if Joseph "will peradventure hate us." With so much guilt, perhaps such a surmise was natural, but it probably was also reflective of the conceptual and affectional inadequacy of Joseph's brethren that they even thought such a thing, after all that Joseph had just done for them.

Those who are large of soul, who have generosity of spirit, are also able to manage the big spiritual ideas and truths that little minds simply cannot handle. It was Paul who said that love is never wasted. Deserved praise in a family is never wasted either. It is not, of course, that the recipients of the love and praise always respond in a manner we might hope. But it still can be said there is never any waste of love because the giver of such love, or such deserved praise, is also truly a beneficiary. The stretching of the soul and the reaching out to others can produce a capacity for generosity that may, in fact, exceed the capacity of the recipient to receive or to appreciate the love or praise given. But love is never wasted because, at a minimum, it enlarges the capacity of the giver; in that sense something good always happens.

One can see in individuals like Hyrum Smith, or Joseph in Egypt, this spirit of generosity, this selflessness, which did not require them to compute beforehand the benefits to them of their actions. Perhaps the individual who is filled with doubt about life's purpose himself uses too much of his psychic energy in processing his doubts, energy that might well be channeled into acts of service. Surely the person who is too caught up in sensual things dispenses too much of his energy, mental and physical, in the realization of self-satisfaction to have much time or thought left for others.

It is noteworthy that some of Lehi's swinging sons and others in that party of immigrants "began to sing, and to speak with much rudeness." (1 Nephi 18:9.) Later Lehi laments that his son Jacob had to suffer "because of the rudeness of thy brethren." (2 Nephi 2:1.) The refining powers of real religion are a great asset in a family or society.

True theology can help us to persist in well-doing, when others grow weary, and to live—despite all frustrations and disappointments—in accordance with the doctrines of Jesus; truth can help us to see beauty in an otherwise ugly world.

Do we doubt, in the context of such case studies, the truth of what General Douglas MacArthur said to Congress, that even our own international problems are "basically theological"?

Unless man can get it straight soon, in terms of the divine truths bequeathed to him in scriptures ancient and modern, mankind's efforts to erect substitute value systems, his efforts to provide a substitute moral momentum, and his efforts to substitute institutions for the family—these efforts are all bound to fail.

Men need to be willing to look unflinchingly, unblinkingly to those things, and those things alone, that have the power to lift man and to save him. The agnostic needs to think the "unthinkable," and the doubter needs to have the courage to doubt doubt.

Someone has said, "What good is parent education if it is not clear what the curriculum is?" Of course, there are tactical skills we need in families and in all our interpersonal relations. But even good tactics, in the absence of over-all strategy, win only battles, not wars. If we are only temporary brothers, then we become, in a sense, obstacles to each other, things to be used in another's search for satisfactions. We are eternal brothers, and earthly parents are trustees of the children of our Father in heaven. What more important task can we possibly have?

Men and women have as much individuality as do individual snowflakes, no two of which, we are told, are ever quite alike. Indeed, the democracy of death may blind us to the aristocracy of achievement. All men ultimately die, but the accumulated "luggage" they take with them into the next great adventure is so different. Should we who see differences in babies so soon after their birth not expect variety in each human snowflake after the resurrection? There is really only one thing that grinds away those different configurations in character: sin.

Snowflakes, though different, are of the same substance. So it is with man. We are the begotten spirit children of our Father in heaven with endless variety in the configurations of our personalities. But the thing that we have in common is that we are the spirit offspring of our Father in heaven, and in his infinite wisdom he has provided his Only Begotten Son—in the flesh, our elder brother and friend, Jesus—to lead us back home.

Man's search for such bedrock purpose and for core values will be a search in vain if it searches for new answers, or if it moves in the direction of false religion or merely in the direction of political ideology. These will prove to be only conceptual *cul de sacs,* not the solitary path to happiness.

The reality to which we must look is the truth, in its

fullest sense, contained in the gospel of Jesus Christ. Is it likely that mankind can save itself, when the answer is so simple and so obvious?

The Book of Mormon speaks of that incident in the Old Testament when Moses lifted up a brazen serpent in the wilderness that all who had been bitten by the fiery serpents might look upon it and thereby live. But as the Book of Mormon concludes:

> *But few understood the meaning of those things, and this because of the hardness of their hearts. But there were many who were so hardened that they would not look, therefore they perished. Now the reason they would not look is because they did not believe that it would heal them. (Alma 33:20.)*

Many today do not believe, of their problems, that the gospel of Jesus Christ will heal them. But they are wrong. Many today are so hardened that they will not even look, but one day their knees, too, will bow in acknowledgment that Jesus is the Christ.

Again, the issue is the importance of being able to believe in the truth in order to do the most realistic thing to spare us present pain and spiritual death.

Symbolically and actually, the Son of God has been lifted up upon the cross, and it is to him that we look so that we might "live, even unto that life which is eternal."

Each family, properly established, can help itself and others to do that simple thing.

The Lord has said, ". . . establish a house, even a house of prayer, a house of fasting, a house of faith, a house of learning, a house of glory, a house of order, a house of God." (D&C 88:119.) Though this scripture referred to the School of the Prophets, every home ought to be a mini-school of the prophets, since so much learning can occur there. Indeed, so much learning (good or bad) does occur in a family whether we wish it to or not. It is simply a question of how righteously influential we want our family school to be. Family standards are the criteria by which we measure other important things too: ". . . only men to whom the family is sacred will ever have a standard or a status by which to criticise the state." (G. K. Chesterton, *Everlasting Man,* p. 146.)

To delight in the achievements of other members of the family prepares us to delight in the achievements of others in life, even in the achievements of one's competitors. "It isn't necessary to blow another person's light in order to let your own light shine." (Anonymous.) For people who like light, the more light the merrier!

The Homer ("Pug") Warner family was one in which the children saw each other in a most pleasing way. When two children had hoped for a pair of boots (and there wasn't money for two pairs), the son who didn't get the boots was truly thrilled for his brother who did. That family still rallies around each other in the same manner, taking joy vicariously in the achievements of each other. But that trait did not come to that family after they had all married and set up their own families. It was part of the luggage each child took with him or her. (For this touching story, see "Christmas Is for Sharing," by Richard Warner, *Improvement Era,* November 1970, p. 140.)

Sometimes it is our very commitment to family and our deep desire to be friends, as well as parents, that creates an artificial anxiety that gets in the way of our achieving the very outcomes for which we strive. Family life is real; it is earnest. It does involve mistakes and, in most families, some conflict. There are many reasons for artificial anxiety.

Sometimes as parents, for instance, when we sound "general quarters," it isn't because the enemy has been sighted, but rather, because we have a need to demonstrate to the "crew" that the "captain" is on the bridge.

Jesus, on the other hand, was never angry because of a wrong that was done to him, but rather, he saw the sin in the other person as a deep, unmet need in the life of that person to which he, as Jesus, *had* to respond for the sake of the other individual. Often our egos get bruised and our reactions are based partly on principle and partly on personal pique.

Sometimes as parents we feel too obligated to react to every blip on the radar scope. If we choose that as a parental style, we will find ourselves engaged in almost perpetual parental arbitration and litigation. The United States Supreme Court often tries to pick only those cases that it truly wants to influence and affect, leaving alone most decisions that have already been made (even though the Justices might like to confirm or upset some of these).

While some crises need to be dealt with immediately, there are those challenges and those questions that can properly be deferred until later in the interest of having greater effectiveness in our responses. Sometimes the very best time to discuss a disturbing habit or trait on the part of a member of the family is not when that trait has just been exhibited, but later. When there is no immediate issue involved, there is often a better chance to have mutual consideration of the challenge, free of the jarring emotions that so often accompany the immediate crisis. Wise crisis management, therefore, does not always mean the immediate resolution of the crisis.

Balance needs to be struck with regard to parental style in the matter of dealing with issues that occur in the family setting. If, for instance, parents in their desire to avoid conflict don't deal promptly enough with unpleasant things, then something is being unwisely repressed that may be returned sevenfold later on. The child, for instance, who feels that he is being dealt with unjustly needs to have closure concerning such a matter. On the other hand, parents who feel they must hold court all the time, on every issue, will do nothing but hold court, finding little time for friendship.

We, as parents, would also do well to hold one partner and/or some of ourselves in reserve so that we are not entirely spent on tactical matters. Strategic reserves are intended to be just that: something held in reserve for the moments that are decisive. If both parents commit themselves simultaneously to the field of action on every issue, as a pair, they will miss those opportunities when it is wise to have one parent held in reserve so that if the other parent, in a sense, has spent himself, or herself, there is still someone left to shape the final outcome; sometimes parents need to pass the baton, so to speak, so that one of them is fresh for the next lap.

It is a disciplined as well as a sweet family, indeed, in which the members thereof have learned to forgo in order to meet the needs of another individual. This capacity is especially needed when members of the family should forget their own immediate needs to rally around another member of the family who is in distress or who is in the process of a special achievement. This quality also determines a family's capacity to hold back, individually, in order that some larger, collective objective may be achieved.

For most families, all of this means more trying, followed by some failing—which then needs to be followed by forgiving and forgetting. In most families, this means, too,. the setting of more realistic expectations about what can be achieved. A family with small children that leaves in a crowded station wagon for a vacation with the hope that there will be no spats and difficulties may be naive. Some families may achieve this, but often even healthy families may be only a few miles on their way to a vacation when sibling conflict arises and then unfortunate self-fulfilling prophecies get made and regrets are expressed about "Why did we ever come on this trip anyway?" The expectation of a Camelot in a crowded car is not usually realistic. In such situations, it is often better to let the "lower courts" solve certain matters and not have a "supreme court" that is too judicially active. Otherwise, regrets developed in such situations may exceed the "crime."

We are expected not only to endure each other, but to endure well and gladly. In some situations simply hanging on happily is a good part of the task to be achieved. Grace under pressure can be contagious. Seeing other members of the family cope well under pressure lets the rest of the family know that it can be done. Just as importantly, the member of the family who endures well is able to do that (even though his cause is just) because he or she is selfless.

One would scarcely expect to become an able trial lawyer without ever having gone into the courtroom. True, some men enter the courtroom with basically better equipment than others and once there some learn faster than others. But no one enters the drama and the pressures of arbitration, fact-finding, and conflict without learning something from that experience, even at the expense of a little suffering. In the administration of justice in our families, where love and law first come together, we should not expect to engage in that high adventure without seeing mistakes made, some bigger than others, and without seeing some failures. Most mothers occasionally have to wipe a tear or two from an eye. Most fathers have those moments when they might feel somewhat unappreciated. Most children see and feel things their parents might have handled just a little bit better.

The importance of righteous reciprocity is given to us by the Lord when he says of his next coming that he "shall come to recompense unto every man according to his work, and measure unto every man according to the measure which he had measured to his fellow man." (D&C 1:10.) The idea of metered justice is intriguing. Those who have been generous and selfless in their relations with others have large conduits through which their love, affection, and justice quickly pass to their fellowmen. But those who are ungenerous have small-bore conduits that are also twisted, so that even that small portion which they mete out to their fellowmen comes slowly and laboriously.

The administration of justice and judgment in family life is surely that place where we do so much to determine the diameter of those same conduits through which we communicate love, esteem, and justice to our fellowmen. Family life, better than anything else, can widen these conduits and keep them cleaned out too.

Grandparenthood is often characterized by perspective and poise that some parents lack. Grandparents don't suddenly stop caring simply because the immediate generation for which they felt responsible has now moved out from under their roof. They continue to empathize, to care, and to counsel, and they should, for their influence is needed. Grandparents are often the strategic reserve who can overlook dirty clothes and untied shoelaces and sibling rivalries—not because they fail to see such, but rather, because their unconditional love for their grandchildren is so irrepressible. Grandparents have usually experienced enough peaks and valleys with offspring so that they do not overreact and also so that they don't get overinvolved.

The shortfalls, in relation to both gospel standards and

101

our own expectations, will come to most of us. Picking ourselves up smilingly as we learn a lesson is an experience through which most parents, as well as children, must go. Sometimes this "recovery" must be done in full view of the family, and, then, there is no larger audience than the family. It is an audience that is at once both loving and intimidating.

There is something about the very act of trying again—whether by parent or son or daughter—that is one part determination and one part affection, that is one part an appeal for help and one part assertion of adequacy. To such efforts, in and out of family life, how vital it is that we give, facially and verbally, our acknowledgment that is also our applause.

Finally, if we can move through crowded lobbies and not notice the jostling elbows of the indifferent, can we not, at least some of the time, take no thought for the elbows at home?

Besides, as Wendell Johnson has warned, ". . . nothing fails like failure. . . . The tears which it produces water the soil from which it grows ever more luxuriantly." (*People in Quandaries,* New York: Harper Brothers, 1946, p. 12.) Some of us are simply too busy irrigating!

CHAPTER NINE

All Family Duties

*R*eal Zions have been achieved at several points in history. Such models can be intimidating unless the model is, in a sense, dangled before us, and unless we realize that such an achievement is significantly possible, we are apt to leave off even trying. But let us look at the model.

Long before there was such a society as the city of Enoch, the Lord prepared Enoch. (See Moses 6.) Enoch later stood in relation to his people as a father stands in relation to his family. Significantly, Enoch was "but a lad" when he was asked to deal with his hostile host culture in which "all the people hate me." Further, Enoch was, like Moses, "slow of speech." But the Lord's Spirit was upon him, and the Lord compensated for his frailties just as the Lord can for each of us as fathers or mothers if his Spirit "is upon us."

Next the Lord blessed Enoch with a special vision, with a special perspective, concerning things "which were not visible to the natural eye." Enoch became a seer. Fathers may not be anointed quite so dramatically, nor see as far or as deeply as

Enoch saw, but they can have inspiration and the sweet perspective of the gospel about "the spirits which God had created" and placed within the home over which the father presides. Enoch confronted a disbelieving society with a simple inquiry, "Why counsel ye yourselves, and deny the God of heaven?" So many in the world make the mistake of counseling themselves and denying the God of heaven from whom they should receive counsel.

The message that Enoch gave that faltering society within which many finally hearkened to his words involves the same basic first principles of the gospel that we as parents in our time are asked by our Father in heaven to teach our children: to believe and repent, to be baptized, and to receive the gift of the Holy Ghost. Enoch urged his society to teach their children that everyone must repent or they can in no wise inherit the kingdom of God. Enoch said, "Teach these things freely unto your children," and then he described the fall and the atonement, the heartland principles of the gospel that pertain to the plan of salvation.

The experiences of Enoch are dramatic events in which he led his people to a condition of righteousness. (See Moses 7.) This group reached a point where "the Lord called his people Zion, because they were of one heart and one mind, and dwelt in righteousness; and there was no poor among them." Then, and only then, came the building of the city of holiness, even Zion. His family of faithful finally had to be separated from "the residue of the people" who were unresponsive to the message. So, in today's world, fathers and mothers will need to teach their children with sufficient and special effectiveness so that they are not contaminated by "the residue of the people."

Enoch pressed God as to why God wept over the "residue of the people." Then we are given a marvelous insight concerning God: "The Lord said unto Enoch: Behold these thy brethren; they are the workmanship of mine own hands, and I gave unto them their knowledge, in the day I created them; and in the Garden of Eden, gave I unto man his agency."

God then goes on to reconstruct how he has given commandments to those he has created and to whom he has given agency, that they "should love one another, and that they should choose me, their Father." But God then laments the fact that "the residue of the people" are "without affection and they hate their own blood."

Note how this description of "the residue of the people" parallels the description in the ninth chapter of Moroni in which a later people were described therein as having fallen so far that they were in a condition in which they "had lost their love one towards another," and they also were "past feeling." The absence of affection and the loss of love—whether in a family or a nation—appear to mark points of almost no return.

That God, who knew the promise and potential of man, wept seeing this great tragedy, this trauma, should be no surprise to us. That there should be a city like the city of Enoch, full of marvelous people in existence at the very same time when the "residue of the people" were described as being so wicked that "there has not been so great a wickedness as among thy brethren among all the workmanship of mine hands," is a necessary reminder for our time about how often righteousness and gross wickedness exist simultaneously, not in the same person, but in the same society. The sharp contrasts no doubt sharpened the choices.

(Parenthetically, while it may be true that the physical body can work against itself in isometrics to promote some physical conditioning [we pit strength and sinew in one part of the body against strength and sinew in another], there is no equivalent of that outcome when we war against ourselves in matters involving spiritual and attitudinal things. In the latter case, we get not added strength, but schizophrenia.)

Enoch's appreciation for the divine empathy of God gives us a clue to the character of Enoch. When Enoch was told by God why God wept, ". . . wherefore Enoch knew, and looked upon their wickedness, and their misery, and wept and stretched forth his arms, and his heart swelled wide as eternity; and his bowels yearned; and all eternity shook." (Moses 7:41.)

So great was the compassion of Enoch for his faltering brethren when he foresaw the episode of Noah and the ark that Enoch said, "I will refuse to be comforted; but the Lord

said unto Enoch: Lift up your heart, and be glad; and look."
(Moses 7:44.)

In speaking of our time, before he closes out that marvelous vision given to Enoch, God describes how he will send forth truth:

> . . . out of the earth, to bear testimony of mine Only
> Begotten; his resurrection from the dead; yea, and
> also the resurrection of all men; and righteousness
> and truth will I cause to sweep the earth as with a
> flood, to gather out mine elect from the four quarters
> of the earth, unto a place which I shall prepare, an
> Holy City, that my people may gird up their loins,
> and be looking forth for the time of my coming; for
> there shall be my tabernacle, and it shall be called
> Zion, a New Jerusalem. (Moses 7:62.)

Latter-day revelations to Joseph Smith also describe the judgments of Almighty God that shall come upon the earth prior to that culminating scene, and emphasize that "men's hearts shall fail them." But long before, Enoch was similarly advised that these times of tribulation in latter days would be times when men's hearts would be "failing them."

Throughout all of this, there are a number of things that are of striking importance: the humility of Enoch, who was, like Moses, weak and/or slow of speech; the righteousness of Enoch, which gave him access to the Spirit; gospel perspectives, which permitted Enoch to keep his head when those about him were losing theirs. All these and other insights combine to suggest how important it is for us as individuals, and particularly as parents, to be able to teach our children, by the power of the Spirit, the fundamental and simple truths they need to know in order to be able to survive spiritually.

When groups of people have been able to establish especially happy conditions at those few points in human history, it is significant that the descriptions used of these special societies are so strikingly parallel. They are described as having, economically, "all things common among them." There were apparently no "rich and poor, bond and free"; they were all "partakers of the heavenly gift," qualifying for the full operation of the gift of the Holy Ghost in their lives. (4 Nephi 1:3.)

In a Zion there is "no contention . . . because of the love of God which [dwells] in the hearts of the people"; "no envyings, nor strifes, nor tumults, nor whoredoms, nor lyings, nor murders, nor any manner of lasciviousness," and, as a result, "surely there could not be happier people among all the people who [had] been created by the hand of God." (4 Nephi 1:15-16.)

Insofar as a family can become a little Zion, it must stretch toward these same dimensions in its life.

Lest these examples sound altogether too intimidating, too out of reach, it may be worth remembering that in those few instances where individuals or groups so progressed, they reached that point (as in the case of Enoch) only after great efforts. No magic wand was waved over a people to transform them suddenly.

Rather than having any special techniques (perhaps there were such, but the scriptures are quite silent on this point), it appears to be the case that the individuals involved simply needed to accept and apply the fundamental truths of the gospel and keep the commandments. Then the celestial symptoms began to appear. There apparently is something about accepting wholeheartedly the basic doctrines of the kingdom that permits us to put other things in their proper place.

One does not read, for instance, of people in any scriptural history becoming fascinated with peace *per se* and pursuing it successfully apart from everything else. Rather, one reads of people who accept and apply certain gospel truths and then—not first—comes peace.

There is a truth here that one approaches tremblingly. It is this: that the ordering of the inner man (so he can have happiness in this world and exaltation in the world to come) does not require the acquisition of sophisticated skills and techniques. Rather, the inner change that makes the outer Zion possible depends, first and finally, on our ability to accept and to apply the simple, basic principles of the gospel. When there is righteousness at the core of our soul, then the rippling outward produces situations in which there is no poverty, nor contention, nor lying, nor lasciviousness; there is happiness.

The gospel of Jesus Christ could scarcely be a gospel for all people if, in fact, only the elite could somehow make it work. It is the very simplicity of the gospel that makes the proferred exaltation democratic in terms of its availability. But the democracy of opportunity is followed by an aristocracy of achievement. An aristocracy of saints is, after all, the only safe aristocracy. Membership in that aristocracy is open to all.

Now this is not to say that there are not appropriate tactics or appropriate how-to skills that go with family life, but these skills and techniques and how-to insights are really useful only if the fundamental things are already in place. Without fundamental commitment to the basic gospel principles, no techniques will, in the end, make any real difference.

A father who truly loves his children, and who is truly striving, for instance, to become a better man, sends off to his children all kinds of messages, in a variety of ways, that lets them know he loves them and that he is a serious disciple of Jesus Christ. Then his children can more easily forgive him the tactical errors, because his basic message is intact: he believes in God and he cares for his family. On the other hand, for the father who is not truly serious in his discipleship, no number of compensatory techniques or humanistic sentiments can ever compensate for the failure of that father to teach the truth by precept and by example.

President Marion G. Romney, in a talk to his General Authority colleagues in January 1969 (after a re-reading of the Doctrine and Covenants), listed the following duties of family and individual members outlined by the Lord. Significantly, President Romney placed the divine declarations into the following categories:

1. Relationship to the Lord
2. Activities within the Church
3. Relationship with others (at home, with neighbors, with enemies, and civic responsibilities)
4. Personal conduct

Scripture is more than a mere recitation of words, and there are more implications behind such divine guidelines than we first imagine. Thus, what follows are those duties categorized by President Romney, along with some efforts by the author (in parentheses) to suggest a few important dimensions of some of these individual and family duties.

1. Relationship to the Lord

a. *"Thou shalt love the Lord thy God with all thy heart, with all thy might, mind, and strength; and in the name of Jesus Christ . . . serve him."*

(Our capacity to love, correctly focused on God and our fellowmen, is the foundation for everything else, for all the law and the prophets still hang on the first two commandments. Such love of God, in the name of Jesus Christ—first felt, first seen, first heard in the home—is tantamount to tilting the trajectory of an individual's life so that he can speed safely home to his Eternal Father.)

b. *"Search the scriptures."*

(Scripture-reading parents are apt to produce scripture-reading children. Institutionalizing the reading of "these commandments" is apt to instill in children a continuing thirst and hunger, and what is at first a duty can later become a delight.)

c. *"Treasure these things up in your hearts, and let the solemnities of eternity rest upon your minds."*

(Scriptures are often stored away for later retrieval when they are more relevant. To whom is awe more natural than a child? When a child or teenager sees parents filled with wonder, it is no more necessary to explain all the doctrinal details than it is to immediately describe the geologic detail of the Grand Canyon when it first bursts into view. There are times when exclamation surpasses explanation.)

d. *"Let all men beware how they take my name in their lips."*

(In a world filled with rudeness and clever denunciations of Deity, some of us must reassert the holiness of the name of God. Profane parents will probably produce profane children, and, ironically, if there is no respect for God, there is seldom real respect for his children, our fellowmen.)

f. *"Confess the hand of God in all things."*

(Though men in their agency are sinful and destructive,

109

God is never surprised; his plans roll forward, involving cata-
clysmic destruction but ultimately also loving redemption for
all who will. The true and living God is no detached Deity, but
a Father whose Only Begotten Son took his five wounds at the
front of the fray.)

g. *"Thank the Lord thy God in all things."*

(In giving thanks for their daily bread, families can constitute cultural counterpoint to the swelling chorus of
secularism that asks not for daily bread, but for a guaranteed
lifetime of leisure and plenty. The one life-style features gratitude, the other a demanding growl.)

h. *"Continue in prayer and fasting."*

(Just as some evil can not be excised but by prayer and
fasting, so some family and individual challenges require of us
extra efforts that feature fasting as well as praying.)

i. *"Be patient in afflictions."*

(Patience is a part of the act of sensible submittal to God,
for a saint is "as a child, submissive, meek, humble, patient,
full of love, willing to submit to all things which the Lord seeth
fit to inflict upon him." Francis Bacon reminds us that "prosperity doth best discover vice but adversity doth best discover
virtue.")

j. *"In days of sorrow, call upon the Lord."*

(Though some prayers ought to be prayers of adoration
and appreciation without petition, we do need to petition for
relief, and the family that can kneel together without bitterness in times of sorrow is usually a family that can cope with
both adversity and prosperity.)

k. *"Lift up your hearts and rejoice."*

(Often in a world pervaded with pessimism, the home can
be the source of hope. Despair is an acquired reflex, but once
acquired it is like a dandelion: it needs so little soil or encouragement to sprout afresh. The regular relapses into despair and
doubt of ancient Israel in Sinai are a good example of this.)

l. *"Be of good cheer before my face."*

(The "good cheer" of the disciple is not naivete but reality.
Paul said, "We are troubled on every side, yet not distressed;
we are perplexed, but not in despair; persecuted, but not forsaken; cast down, but not destroyed." [2 Corinthians 4:8-9.]

Cheer is contagious hope, that vital third strand to be weaved together with faith and charity.)

2. Activities Within the Church

a. *Receive the words of the President of the Church as if they were spoken by the Lord God himself.*

(Living prophets can and do under inspiration particularize for an age or era when there are often the equivalents of Red Seas to be parted and crossed; the prophet shows the way and the saints will obey!)

b. *"Meet together often to partake of" the sacrament.*

(When attendance at sacrament meeting is "the thing to do," such loving reinforcement by a family will last long after children leave the family's immediate influence. Since the sacramental prayer is one of the few fixed prayers we offer [perhaps because in the simplicity of those repeated words we can most accurately recovenant and be reminded of the gift of the atonement, whereas *laissez-faire* prayers could lead us away from simple, accurate reminders of that grand act], we need to participate regularly in the partaking of the sacrament.)

c. *"Teach one another the doctrine of the kingdom."*

(What better setting to do this is there than in the home?)

d. *"Seek diligently to turn the hearts of the children to their fathers, and the hearts of the fathers to the children."*

(We have often and fittingly used this exhortation to bolster our efforts in genealogical and temple work, but another dimension of its application could be the family home evening. President Harold B. Lee said, "I would have you consider seriously whether or not that binding with your family will be secure if you have waited until you have passed beyond the veil before your hearts then yearn for your children whom you have neglected to help along the way. It is time for us to think of turning the hearts of parents to children now while living, that there might be a bond between parents and children that will last beyond death. It is a very real principle, and we should consider it." [*Ensign,* February 1971, p. 11.])

3. *Pay tithing.*

(Parental example, especially in economic stress, is eloquent example. See President Romney's recollection regarding tithing on pages 51-52.)

f. *"Let every man esteem his brother as himself."*

(Since self-esteem and esteem of others are so connected, the commencement of keeping this commandment occurs in the home, for if there can be esteem in the midst of elbows at home, there can usually be esteem elsewhere.)

g. *"Consecrate of thy properties for the support of the poor."*

(The payment of fast offerings and the children's awareness of a mother in the midst of compassionate service can do so much to establish sensitivity to poverty and also provide experience in actually responding thereunto, however modestly.)

h. *"Let every man learn his duty, and to act in the office in which he is appointed, in all diligence."*

i. *"Arise and shine forth, that thy light may be a standard for the nations.*

(A fine family can be a light and standard for a neighborhood.)

3. Relationship with Others

a. *In the home:* "Set in order your own house." (A family is not only the first but it is also the best place to help individuals strike a balance between order and freedom.)

"Have your children blessed in church by the elders." (So, too, a father's blessing later for each of his children can be a milestone in the life of each son and daughter.)

b. *With neighbors:* "Thou shalt not covet." "Cease to find fault one with another." "Love thy neighbour as thyself." "It becometh every man who hath been warned to warn his neighbor." "If thou shalt find that which thy neighbour has lost, thou shalt make diligent search till thou shalt deliver it to him again." (This is another specific manifestation of the commandment to love one's neighbor, which, in today's world of lessened concern for property, is much in need of revival.) "Forgive one another." "Cease to contend . . . with" or "speak evil" of "another." "Love," and "impart one to another as the gospel requires." "Thou shalt pay for that which thou shalt receive of thy brother."

c. *With one's enemies:* "Be not afraid of your enemies," and don't get in debt to them. "Make unto yourselves friends with the mammon of unrighteousness. . . . Leave judgment alone with me."

d. *Civic responsibilities:* "Renounce war and proclaim peace." Elect to office good and wise men. Obey and befriend "that law which is the constitutional law of the land."

4. Personal Conduct

Live not "after the manner of the world." Be diligent. "Seek learning, even by study and also by faith." "Thou shalt not be idle." Be thrifty. "Be anxiously engaged in a good cause." "Cease to sleep longer than is needful." "Retire to thy bed early." "Arise early."

Abstain from the use of wine, tobacco, strong and hot drinks. Eat meat sparingly and remember wheat for man. Do not covet. Do not boast. "Beware of pride." Seek not the praise of the world. Be meek and humble. "Observe the Sabbath day to keep it holy."

"Purify your hearts and cleanse your hands." "Cast away your idle thoughts and your excess of laughter." "Cease to be unclean." "Practice virtue and holiness . . . continually." "Clothe yourselves with the bond of charity."

"Live by every word that proceedeth forth from the mouth of God." Be faithful unto death.

In a family or in a society where these unglamorous commands are taken seriously (however small may be the numbers of those involved), there will be a Zion in progress. When we avoid living "after the manner of the world," we can avoid many of the world's problems. For instance, in America alcoholism is the biggest health problem after heart disease and cancer: Half the murders in America involve individuals who have been drinking; drinkers are seven times more likely to be separated or divorced; alcoholism may cost as much as $15 billion a year; and at least half of each year's highway harvest in car accidents are traceable to drinking. (See *Time,* April 22, 1974.) Yet most teenagers who drink are following parental example. How grateful we should be for the celestial counsel to abstain from alcohol!

We really do not need to become parental technicians, but to accept and apply the fundamental commandments. Human variety exists—and apparently will persist; however, we must come together, uniformly, as to the commandments and as to doctrine. One disciple may prefer the color of purple and another green; one believer may prefer a career in dentistry and another in farming. But both need repentance.

Parental style matters, of course, but parental substance matters more. One good parent might be inclined to teach more often by the lecture method, whereas another parent might be more inclined to involve his children participatively. *What* these parents should teach, however, must remain constant, for it is fixed for all eternity.

We can expect much variety in the kingdom and in the family concerning the things that are not fundamental, but concerning the things that really matter, we shall find that the parent-saints are incredibly alike.

If techniques and tactical things were not just important, but also crucial, surely God would have told us so.

We also can learn so much in a family about duty itself and can often be moved by a sense of duty when the mind will not urge us on and when energies ebb. So often the hills of family life that we have to climb require us simply to put one foot in front of the other, not because we may see at any moment a breathtaking panorama that explains why a particular challenge had to be met, or why an obstacle had to be in our path, but rather because we have had too many great experiences and too many consolatory consequences in the past by simply doing our duty to dare not to do it now.

One cannot forget the image painted by Dostoevsky of the willingness some humans have to mount the cross for mankind —but only under certain conditions. They would mount the cross if everyone was looking on, applauding, and if so, they could then be done with service to mankind, whereas love, as that same Dostoevsky reminded us, is "a completely patient science." So is parenthood!

Family life is a situation in which we must perpetually renew our sense of brotherhood. Some may feel that for us to be judged in terms of our success, or lack of success, in the home is an unfair judgment based on too small a segment of life. These brief mortal years are surely tiny in relationship to all that has gone before our birth. Consider, however, the marvels of technology to see what can be done with, for instance, microfiche in which many printed pages can be reduced to single dots. (Indeed, the whole Bible can be reduced to a series of dots on a piece of plastic no more than an inch and a half square.) Just as one of these dots can be enlarged to become a whole printed page to be examined and scrutinized (though the dot is ever so small), mortality is a kind of microfiche. Life is a dot of time that, when examined carefully by God's divinely discerning eye, tells all that needs to be known about how we have coped, failed, and succeeded in the experiences of life.

When we read the Lord's list of "all family duties," each duty becomes a challenge. The scriptural insights about idleness and about having healthy attitudes about work are first responded to, or often not at all, in family life.

There is apparently something about idleness that represents a slackening of control on ourselves, something that can stir and revive slumbering bad habits. It isn't simply a question of our being kept too busy to sin, though that is a practical and useful deterrent at times. Idleness seems to let the soul sag (the captain leaves the bridge, the sentries sleep, and the pirates come on board).

We are not talking here, of course, about active contemplation or well-directed leisure, but that idleness which, in a sense, can start a soul slide.

One is tempted to ask: Can we not be trusted to have idleness and time on our hands? The answer is, probably not—any more than we can usually be trusted with riches or to cope with situations where there is gross unchastity all about us and still expect to come out unscathed. (For in such latter situations, even with abstinence the eyes and the mind record footage that can later be used against us.)

When we recognize that what we are really engaged in in this instance is war against evil, the more important the simple strategies are, like occupying and holding high ground, and refusing to go into the swamps simply to see if we could survive.

There are simply too many bleached bones lying about the landscape as haunting reminders of the importance of fleeing from the terrain of temptation. Sometimes circumstances may cast up an unavoidable encounter with things we would rather not brush against, but in each of these we have been promised by the Lord that even then he will make an escape passage for us.

Meanwhile, one ought not to run the risks of bravado in our behavior, for bravado and boredom have brought on so much sadness.

Families can encourage individuals to act with initiative in their own framework of responsibilities. On one occasion the Prophet Joseph Smith wrote to some of his colleagues as follows:

> *There are many things of much importance, on which you ask counsel, but which I think you will be perfectly able to decide upon, as you are more conversant with the peculiar circumstances than I am; and I feel great confidence in your united wisdom; therefore you will excuse me for not entering into detail. If I should see anything that is wrong, I would take the privilege of making known my mind to you, and pointing out the evil.* (Teachings of the Prophet Joseph Smith, *p. 176*.)

Such a style in a prophet or in parents can produce growth in the context of wise experience and trust.

Families can also help us establish a sort of balance of trade in the matters of giving and taking, of erring and forgiving, in a world in which people tend to demand too little of themselves and too much of others. Establishing a sense of balance and proportion about what one can expect of himself and of others is so fundamental. Family life can do much to let one at least know that there are certain limitations, certain boundary lines, beyond which his demands may not appropriately push. Family life can help us to experience what the consequences of reaching too far are, since, in taking turns, we usually learn what it is like to be on the receiving end of someone who demands too much—and such learning costs us much less than the same lessons learned later.

We are told that he that "keepeth a commandment with a slothful heart" is neither fully complying nor growing. They who do not receive a gift gladly fail not only to enjoy that gift, but also "that which they might have received." (D&C 88:32-33.) One's style of giving and receiving is, as with so many things, shaped in the home.

Apparently the recurring challenge is to do things at the right time, for the right reasons, in the right spirit, and in the right way. Then there can be full closure in terms of human growth. Otherwise, though transactions may occur, though a ritual may transpire, a real spiritual outcome has not been achieved. How crucial the training in family life can be in this respect!

Another small tendency that runs through many of our lives is the inclination to pass it along when we have been disappointed or offended. Remember the line from *Fiddler on the Roof,* the one where the beggar observes that just because the potential donor had a bad day was no reason why the beggar should have a bad day. To stop what could be a negative chain reaction is a generous thing to do in the daily marketplace of living. Children who have parents who, even most of the time, refuse to "pass it along" are blessed indeed, for they will know from firsthand experience that we do not need to be mere relay transmitters at home, at school, at play.

The crucial, redemptive human response does not begin with legislation to abolish poverty by a parliament, but in the empathy and compassion we learn in a parlor. It begins with the necessity of changing individuals who, once they take seriously the commandment to love the Lord their God and their fellowmen, will not abide the existence of poverty but will move to eradicate it—but in the Lord's lasting way, using the principles of the gospel. The ninety-nine will not only refuse to rest while one sheep is lost, but they will also feed that sheep when they find him.

Our successes are a challenge, too. So often in life even deserved exhilaration does not go uninterrupted for long. Rude reminders of other realities press in upon us. Perhaps this is because the adversary probes for vulnerability even in our victories; perhaps it occurs because some blessings are also a challenge. It may be that just as large doses of power, wealth, and leisure are bad for the soul, so is uninterrupted exhilaration.

Sometimes the interventions are implicit in the joy or success; other times, the reminder comes at the very point of achievement.

What we must realize is that in God's scheme, a point of achievement is often also a departure point; many finish lines are also fresh starting lines. It is as if Sisyphus finally did roll his troublesome boulder to the top of the mountain and paused, perspiringly, but as he wiped the sweat from his eyes, saw that he was not on top at all, but on a plateau from which he must now push on further.

It is a wise individual who can not only delay gratification as a sign of maturity, but who can also project consequences—positive and negative—as a means of behaving with appropriate anticipation. Our homes, therefore, can be little Zions in which we can, initially on a small scale, learn to wait and to project consequences. Out of such homes will come those individuals who can fashion the larger Zion, that special culture that will one day dominate this globe.

An endless chain of happy consequences can flow out of the correct and consciously chosen way of life, but it is a way of life best observed, best taught, best experienced in a family. For out of such families can come the carriers of the celestial culture who are capable of sharing the way with a wider world. These seed bearers and their children will take root in thousands of communities dotting the globe where other men will see the gospel in action.

CHAPTER TEN

Why Counsel Ye Yourselves

*T*hough the scriptural instructions below involve the disciples of Jesus in the Holy Land (and later instructions the Lord gave the early leaders of The Church of Jesus Christ of Latter-day Saints), these have special relevance for parents. Jesus advised the early Twelve that when they were delivered "up to councils" or when they were brought before kings and rulers, they should "take no thought how or what ye shall speak: for it shall be given you in that same hour what ye shall speak. For it is not ye that speak, but the Spirit of your Father which speaketh in you." (Matthew 10:17-20.) This was like a promise the Lord made centuries earlier to Moses, who said, "I am not eloquent." But the Lord reminded him that he, the Lord, would "teach thee what thou shalt say." (Exodus 4:10, 12.) This same promise was made to Jeremiah.

In the latter days we read, "Neither take ye thought beforehand what ye shall say: but treasure up in your minds continually the words of life, and it shall be given you in the

very hour that portion that shall be meted unto every man."
(D&C 84:85.)

As is so often the case, there is a significant addition or
clarification in the latter-day revelation. Clearly we are not
to run around with lazy, blank minds, but we are to "treasure
up in [our] minds continually the words of life," so that we can
draw upon "that portion" that will be needed.

In yet another latter-day revelation, the Lord promises
Joseph Smith and Sidney Rigdon that "it shall be given you
in the very hour, yea, in the very moment, what ye shall say."
(D&C 100:6.)

The point of rehearsing these important scriptures and
episodes involving promises to the Lord's leaders is that surely
God, who has told us how important succeeding in our families
is, will not leave us without parallel blessings and inspiration
in terms of what we should say in our families, especially in
those moments when what we say *really* matters. He will, if
we treasure up proper things in our parental minds, give us
that portion we need to respond to our children. It is, of course,
necessary for us to have the Holy Ghost operating in our lives
to enjoy this blessing.

Since nothing is more important than succeeding in our
families, God will not leave us alone in terms of those prompt-
ings that we need in terms of our vital communications within
our families.

If one wishes to see sobering boldness in action, it has
occurred repeatedly in the presidential messages in the family
home evening manuals published by The Church of Jesus
Christ of Latter-day Saints. In those publications the living
prophets have promised members of the Church that if we have
love in our homes, will gather our families about us, and will
seriously seek to teach, socialize, and spiritualize with them
(as the family home evening program calls for), "Families who
prayerfully and consistently hold their weekly home evenings,
and who work together during the week to apply the lessons in
their lives, will be blessed. There will be better feelings between
husband and wife, between parents and children, and among
children. In such homes the Spirit of the Lord will be made
manifest."

Modern prophets have further stated: ". . . you may be rewarded by a fulfillment of the promise that if the fathers will discharge this responsibility, not one in a hundred of your family . . . would ever go astray."

Finally, these calm but bold assurances include the assertion that if there is love in the home, "should those children thus taught stray away, they would eventually return again, lest they lose their place in the eternal family circle."

These promises are the latter-day equivalent—and much more—of the promise that Malachi gave to ancient Israel with regard to the duty of tithing: ". . . prove me now herewith, saith the Lord of hosts, if I will not open you the windows of heaven, and pour you out a blessing, that there shall not be room enough to receive it." (Malachi 3:10.)

With God as our guide, we have a guide who will never betray us, for "he cannot walk in crooked paths; neither doth he vary from that which he hath said; neither hath he a shadow of turning from the right to the left, or from that which is right to that which is wrong. . . ." (Alma 7:20.)

In this case, latter-day prophets are promising us what is an even greater blessing: that our children, who are our real treasures, will be saved if we will take our relationships with them seriously enough to do specific things and regularize those things in a family life-style. The invitation is insistent about the ultimate spiritual blessings of family life, for the Lord through his anointed has, in effect, said, "prove me now herewith," and has promised to "pour you out a blessing, that there shall not be room enough to receive it."

The theme of using obscure people or obscure situations to carry out his mighty work seems to be an almost leitmotiv with God. He will, for instance, bring The Church of Jesus Christ of Latter-day Saints "out of obscurity" and "out of the wilderness" until it will become "clear as the moon, and fair as the sun, and terrible as an army with banners." (D&C 1:30; 5:14.) He chose an obscure boy to be the sole mortal audience at what was the greatest theophany in the history of this planet—the appearance of the Father and the Son to initiate this dispensation of the fulness of times. That boy lived in an obscure part of an adolescent nation.

Centuries earlier, God chose an obscure village, Bethlehem, in which to have his Only Begotten Son born; the obscure, as well as a despised, town of Nazareth in which to have his Only Begotten Son raised; an obscure part of the world for the resurrection and atonement to be accomplished.

If one wishes to carry this pattern further—on from individuals and towns to a planet—note the words of Archibald MacLeish about our earth: a "small . . . planet . . . of a minor star off at the edge of an inconsiderable galaxy." (*National Geographic,* May 1974, p. 596.) Yet this became the planet on which Jesus was born, lived, taught, established his church, and was crucified—an incredibly obscure point in the swarm of stars and the groups of galaxies.

We, in fact, live on the outer rim of the Milky Way galaxy, which contains a mere 100 billion stars; but that galaxy, appallingly, when compared to its sister galaxies, pales in its spatial significance. It was here, nevertheless, that God chose to do the work of the atonement.

Perhaps this recurring theme is worth some final pondering. Part of the gospel message for us is to realize how marvelous and wonderful God is and what he can do to prepare, if we are willing, the weakest of us to deal with the greatest of challenges.

Thus, his message and plan are scaled in their applicability to make use of even those of us who are obscure people in obscure places, for we are noticed by God and our potentials are not lost upon him. What premortal penchant our holy and divine Father may have had that produces this recurring theme we do not know. But it is there, a reminder that his love and power reach not only in the darkest and most obscure recesses of the universe but also into our hearts, bringing to both places light and love.

Thus, in a world filled with much laboring and striving in parliaments, congresses, agencies, and corporate offices, God's extraordinary work is most often done by ordinary people in the seeming obscurity of a home and family.

May we succeed in spreading the gospel feast so attractively within the walls of our own homes that our families will partake!

Index